Elevation in the Eucharist
its History and Rationale

Elevation in the Eucharist
its History and Rationale

by

T. W. Drury, D.D.

Principal of Ridley Hall, Cambridge, and
Examining Chaplain to the Bishop of Liverpool

WIPF & STOCK · Eugene, Oregon

Wipf and Stock Publishers
199 W 8th Ave, Suite 3
Eugene, OR 97401

Elevation of the Eucharist
Its History and Rationale
By Drury, T. W.
Softcover ISBN-13: 978-1-6667-3523-9
Hardcover ISBN-13: 978-1-6667-9210-2
eBook ISBN-13: 978-1-6667-9211-9
Publication date 9/24/2021
Previously published by Cambridge University Press, 1907

This edition is a scanned facsimile of
the original edition published in 1907.

TO MY WIFE
C. B. D.

PREFACE.

A FEW words must be said as to the origin and purpose of this book. Frequent mention was made, in the evidence given before the recent Royal Commission on Ecclesiastical Discipline, of the elevation of the Bread and Wine immediately after Consecration, and not unfrequently the practice of "elevation" was denied, even where the witness distinctly alleged that some such ceremony had taken place[1]. It further appeared, from the evidence of several of the clergymen who were examined, that this discrepancy arose from a distinction drawn between elevating the elements after consecration so as to make them visible to the people, and the practice of a more moderate elevation, either when taking the paten and chalice into the hands, or at the words "Do this in remembrance of Me."

It is beyond dispute that, whatever name may be assigned to it, both types of this ceremony are now practised in many Anglican churches[2]. Yet there is

[1] This occurred in twenty-seven instances. *Report of Royal Commission on Ecclesiastical Discipline*, p. 36.

[2] See the letters from clergymen published in the *Minutes of Evidence taken before the Royal Commission*. Vols. I.—III.

PREFACE.

an entire absence of any direction in the rubrics to lift up the elements, except so far as is necessary in order to perform those manual acts, which were specified with such deliberate care at the last revision.

In the absence of any rubrical authority, the ceremony is defended on the ground that the "elevation or showing to the people," which was expressly forbidden in the first Prayer Book, had an exclusive reference to the lifting up with a view to worship, which had been introduced after the rise of a belief in Transubstantiation, and is specially referred to in Article XXVIII. Accordingly, other explanations of the purpose of elevation are put forward by those who practise it. Even extreme elevation in view of the congregation is justified as enabling the manual acts to be made visible, when the eastward position is adopted, while a slight elevation is interpreted to signify a presentation to God of the memorial of Christ's sacrifice[1].

These varying accounts suggested a more exact enquiry into the various types of elevation which have been practised in the Church, and into the several shades of meaning which they have been taken to represent. I have endeavoured to collect and arrange the evidence available on the subject, and to present a fair and impartial, if not a complete, statement of the main issues which are involved. I have thought

[1] *Minutes of Evidence*, I. pp. 268, 269, 274, 414, 440, 476, 533, 541: II. pp. 37, 114, 118, &c , &c.

that this might be more useful than a strong expression of my own views upon the whole subject.

Such an enquiry cannot be regarded as unimportant. There is no more striking, and hardly any more significant, ceremony in the Roman Mass than the elevation of the Host. It is the very climax of the service, and is looked for with feelings of the most intense expectation and devotion. Its intention, moreover, is undoubted, and is one which marks distinctly the "line of deep cleavage" between the Churches of England and Rome.

If this study has proceeded on sound lines of enquiry, there can be no doubt as to the historical meaning in the Western Church of any extreme elevation of the elements as soon as they have been consecrated[1]. And however sincerely a different signification may now be intended, the coincidence in time between the Roman elevation, and that recently introduced into the Anglican service, must inevitably result in a serious confusion between the two ceremonies, and in frequent misunderstanding[2].

---

[1] "That the people with all reverence and honour may worship the same." *The Rationale*, see p. 160. *Ut visum ab omnibus adoretur.* Coutances Missal, A.D. 1557. See pp. 110 f.

[2] *Report*, p. 35. "Those who guided the Church of England through this process of restoration to primitive antiquity were of opinion that the elevation was so connected with the repudiated doctrine of Transubstantiation, as distinguished from the Real Presence, that it ought not to be suffered to remain." Extract from a judgment in the Court of the Arches by Sir R. Phillimore.

The significance of elevation cannot therefore be regarded as a matter of private interpretation. We must weigh, with the utmost care, not only its historical purpose, but also the impression produced on the popular mind, when a ceremony, so intimately wrapped up with a doctrine repudiated at the Reformation, is being restored, without authority, at the very point of the service where it is most liable to be misunderstood.

But further, a distinction has been drawn, in the recent Report of the Royal Commission, between extreme elevation to evoke worship, and "the slight lifting up which has come to be practised after consecration at the words 'Do this in remembrance of Me'." The history of elevation, as practised at these words, is a very complicated one, but it does not appear, from any of the evidence adduced in this volume, that moderate elevation had, at this particular point of the service, any peculiar significance other than that of the ordinary post-consecration form. The slighter elevation of the Chalice, which was almost universally enjoined, arose out of special reasons which are definitely named, and not from any variation in the meaning of the ceremony[1].

One witness stated to the Commission that he believed the grounds on which this lesser act of

---

[1] See below, pp. 113—124.

elevation is practised to be "a certain interpretation of τοῦτο ποιεῖτε, 'Do this[1].'" It is obvious that such a view raises a serious doctrinal question, and that the ceremony, when so explained, commits our common worship to a highly controversial interpretation of those words. I am fully aware that such an intention is far from the minds of many who practise this moderate elevation, but the careful employment of the ceremony at that point of the service, as an act of oblation, certainly gives the impression of fixing upon the words τοῦτο ποιεῖτε a meaning, which no formulary of the Church of England sanctions, and which no commentator of the first rank has ever adopted[2]. In a public Liturgy such a result is surely to be deprecated, especially where the ceremony, as so used, has no clear historical support, and no rubrical warrant whatever.

The general conclusion to which I have been led is that, while the forms of elevation which were practised *before* consecration appear to have had, for the most part, a God-ward intention, all elevation *after* consecration has, by almost unanimous testimony, been practised with a view to displaying the hallowed Bread and Wine to the people, either as an invitation to Communion, or, in later times, to evoke their adoration.

[1] *Minutes of Evidence*, II. p. 258.
[2] Prof Bigg, in his *Wayside Studies in Ecclesiastical History*, points out that even the Council of Trent did not adopt this interpretation, p. 170.

The results of this enquiry are published at the suggestion of friends whose judgment I greatly value, and I can only add an expression of my own hope and prayer that they may in some small measure promote a fair and dispassionate consideration of the whole subject, and may eventually contribute towards a reasonable conclusion.

My sincere thanks are due to those friends who have helped me in the work Both the Regius and the Norrisian Professor of Divinity have kindly made several valuable suggestions. The Rev. R Sinker, D.D., and the Rev. G. A. Schneider, M A., have not only given their counsel and advice, but also much patient labour in revising the proof sheets. Nor must I forget the help received in preparing the index and in the tedious work of verification from members of my own family.

Few pages fail to show how much I owe to the learned and painstaking labours of Dr Wickham Legg in his *Tracts on the Mass*, and to the Rev. F. E. Brightman, in his *Eastern Liturgies*.

T. W. D.

CAMBRIDGE,
July, 1907.

CONTENTS.

INTRODUCTION (pp. 1—8).

The relative value of ceremonies—divergent lines of meaning in the case of Elevation, 1—8.

CHAPTER I.

EASTERN LITURGIES (pp. 9—62).

(1) ELEVATION AT THE OFFERTORY. No public elevation, 9.—The *Prothesis*, 10.—Great Entrance, 11.

(2) ELEVATION AT THE WORDS OF INSTITUTION. The exact point of consecration.—Recital of Words of Institution, or *Epiclesis*, 13 —Consecration by the Lord's Prayer, 13 f.—by our Lord's *ipsissima verba*, 16 —Enlargement of His words, 17.—ἐπὶ τῶν ἁγίων χειρῶν.—ἀναβλέψας εἰς τὸν οὐρανόν, 18.—ἀναδείξας τῷ Πατρί, 19.—Corresponding action (even fraction) rare, 20 f.— ἀναδείκνυμι and ἀνάδειξις, 21 f.—St Basil, 23 f.—James of Edessa. —Lit. of Coptic Jacobites, 27.

(3) ELEVATION AT τὰ ἅγια τοῖς ἁγίοις. *Meaning of the phrase* undoubted from the 4th century, 31 f —Evidence of early writers, 33 f.—and of Liturgies, 35 f —Mozarabic use of *Sancta sanctis*, 36 f —Archdeacon Freeman's view, 38 f.—Translations of τὰ ἅγια κ τ.λ., 43.

Meaning of Elevation at these words.—Use of ὑποδείκνυμι etc. in early Writers and Liturgies, 45 f —Two objections to our conclusions.—(1) The Curtains of the *Bema*,—(2) Roman interpretation of the Eastern elevation, 55 f —Eastern elevation compared with the late Roman elevation before Communion, 59 f.

ADDITIONAL NOTE. THE ROMAN ELEVATION, AND USE OF *ECCE AGNUS DEI*, 60—62.

xiv CONTENTS.

CHAPTER II.

WESTERN LITURGIES (pp. **63—138**).

(1) ELEVATION AT THE OFFERTORY. The ceremony late and not universal, **64** —The *Secretæ*, **66**.—Not named in Roman *Ordinary*,—Stages of growth in English and Foreign Missals, **67** f.—Enjoined in *Ritus Celebrandi Missam*, **69**.—The *Rationale*, **70**.—A more comprehensive view of the Offertory-Oblation, **71**.

(2) ELEVATION AT *QUI PRIDIE* AND *SIMILI MODO*. Three acts of elevation in the Canon compared, **73**.—Origin of this elevation in our Lord's own action, **73** f.—The Western ceremony corresponds to the Eastern enlargement of our Lord's words, **74**. —Earliest mention in the *Micrologus* of 11th cent.—Later evidence, **76** f.—English and Foreign Missals —Moderate elevation enjoined to distinguish from later elevation, **80** f.—Omission from Roman Canon, **81**.—Influence of belief in Transubstantiation, **83** f.

(3) ELEVATION AT *OMNIS HONOR ET GLORIA*. Connected with "the crossings," **84** f.—Not expressly named in English Missals, **85**.—A joint elevation of both elements, **86**.—Earliest mention in *Ordines Romani* and Amalarius of 8th and 9th centuries.—Later evidence, **88** f.—Its varied position, **92**.—Its purpose, **93** f.—Absence from English rubrics qualified by popular use, **94** f.—The second Mozarabic elevation compared with the Eastern, and with that at *Omnis honor et gloria*, **96** f.

(4) ELEVATION AFTER THE WORDS OF CONSECRATION Characteristic of the Western (Roman) Church.—Unknown for 1000 years after Christ, **100** f.—Arose in Gaul, as a protest against Berengarius, in the 11th century, **101** f.

(i) *Elevation of the Host.* Earliest mention in *Carthusian Statutes* of the 12th century, **103**.—Accompanied by bell-ringing, **104**.—A result of the dogma of Transubstantiation, **106** —The adoration of the Host, **107**.—Degrees of elevation.—English service-books, **108** f.—Foreign service-books, **110** f.

CONTENTS. xv

(11) *Elevation of the Chalice.* Greater variation of position, **112.**—Use of the words "Hæc (Hoc) quotiescunque etc," **112** f.—Not so general or so marked as that of the Host,—reasons for this, **113** f.—Technical use of the word "elevation," **115.**—English service-books, **116** f.—Foreign service-books, **118** f. —No difference of meaning signified by the special treatment of the Chalice, **123** f.

(5) ELEVATION AT THE COMMUNION OF THE PEOPLE. **124.** Cf. **60—62.**

DEVELOPMENT OF CEREMONIAL AFTER A.D. 1215.

The new elevation accompanied by rapid development of ceremonial, **124** f.—Extreme lifting up.—Bells —Portable lights —Genuflexion, **125** —Mr Edmund Bishop's witness, **126.**—Effect on Reservation, **126** f.—Festival of *Corpus Christi*, **127.**—Service of Benediction,—Growth of genuflexion, **128** f.

ADDITIONAL NOTE A. EVIDENCE OF ENGLISH COUNCILS, **131—133.**

ADDITIONAL NOTE B. THE CONSECRATION IN THE MOZARABIC MISSAL, **133—138.**

CHAPTER III.

THE RATIONALE OF ELEVATION (pp. **139—165**).

Two main ideas involved,—Presentation to God and to the people, **139** f

(*a*) AT THE OFFERTORY. A dedication of gifts to God's service,—Relation of the offerings to the *Eucharistia*, **141** f.

(*b*) AT *QUI PRIDIE* AND *SIMILI MODO*. Original intention that the manual acts should be visible to all, **142** f.—This elevation came to have a God-ward purpose, connected with the blessing of the elements, **143** f.—The sharp distinction between reverence due to the elements *before* and *after* consecration was of later growth, **145** f.—Both elevations before consecration were mainly presentations to God, **147** f.

xvi   CONTENTS.

(c) AFTER THE CLOSE OF, OR AFTER, THE CANON.

(i) *The Eastern Elevation.* An invitation to Communion, **149** f.

(ii) *Mozarabic Elevation. Ut videatur a populo.* Followed by the Nicene Creed, **150**.

(iii) *At the close of the Western Canon.* Evidence less decisive.—Probably intended to exhibit the consecrated elements to the people, **151** f.

(d) IMMEDIATELY AFTER CONSECRATION. Meaning of this elevation undoubted, **158**.—The lifting up of Christ upon the cross, **159** f.—The growth of direct adoration of the elements, **160** f.—Colet's statute for St Paul's School, **161**.—Passage ascribed to Bonaventura, **162** f.—Elevations after consecration intended to be seen by the people, **164**.

(e) AT THE COMMUNION OF THE PEOPLE. Accompanied by *Ecce Agnus Dei.*—This elevation is clearly for exhibition before Communion.—Only enjoined at actual Communion, **165**.

CHAPTER IV.

ELEVATION AND THE BOOK OF COMMON PRAYER
(pp. **166—181**).

Elevation after consecration modified in 1548, **166** f.,—forbidden in 1549,—all mention omitted in 1552, **167** f.—All points of the service, where elevation occurred, are represented in Anglican Office, **168**.—*Omnis honor et gloria* retained, **168** f.

The Offertory. In 1549 Offerings placed on the Holy Table though not elevated,—Words of Memorial, **169** f.—Ceremonies revived in 17th century, **171** f.,—or partly adopted in 1662, **172**.

The Consecration. Revival of the Manual acts in 17th century welcomed by all.—Baxter's Service, **173** f.—General results of revision of 1662, **177** f.

INTRODUCTION.

THE leaders of the Church of England were mainly guided by two principles, when, in the 16th and 17th centuries, they reconstructed her forms of public worship. In the first place stood their appeal to Holy Scripture as the supreme and ultimate authority, and to the judgment of the Primitive Church as the earliest witness to its meaning. In the second place they claimed that each particular or national church had the right to "ordain, change, and abolish" what was "ordained only by man's authority."

What can certainly claim divine appointment is of primary importance and possesses absolute authority. Moreover, the evidence of apostolic use and general acceptance in very early times must have a weight only second to that of divine command.

But rites and ceremonies which lack such authority at once fall into a secondary place, and even widespread adoption and long-established use cannot deprive a church of the right to modify, or even abolish, such practices as rest only on human authority.

Matters of ceremony belong mainly to the class of things non-essential, for the obvious reason that, while certain *rites* of the Church can claim the authority of our Lord and His Apostles, the *ceremonies*, by which those rites are accompanied and which express their meaning, are, with a few conspicuous exceptions, not of primitive origin.

Accordingly, when a ceremony thus falls into a class of things which have only secondary importance, other principles, of less commanding, though of considerable, moment come into play. The Reformers carefully explain these principles in the historical accounts of the two great stages of development (A.D. 1549 and 1662), which form the introductory chapters to our Book of Common Prayer, and more especially in the chapter "Of Ceremonies."

On the one hand, ceremonies, though in themselves not open to objection as significant of erroneous doctrine, may by their "excessive multitude" "more confound and darken, than declare and set forth Christ's benefits unto us." Or again, "the most weighty cause of the abolishment of certain ceremonies" was that they had been "so far abused, partly by the superstitious blindness of the rude and unlearned, and partly by the insatiable avarice of such as sought more their own lucre than the glory of God, that the abuses could not well be taken away, the thing remaining still."

On the other hand, some ceremonial is necessary,

both for "a decent Order and godly Discipline," and also "to stir up the dull mind of man to the remembrance of his duty to God," and granting this, "surely where the old may be well used, there they cannot reasonably reprove the old only for their age."

It is to such firmness in putting away, not only what was distinctly significant of erroneous teaching, but also what was excessive and liable to abuse, coupled with a deep strong reverence for antiquity, and a firm resolve to maintain the continuity of Church life and order, that we owe that Book of Common Prayer which has for 350 years been "accepted and approved by all sober, peaceable and truly conscientious sons of the Church of England." (Introductory chapters to the *Book of Common Prayer*.)

In view of this, and of the fact that many ceremonies are now being practised which have no rubrical authority, the liturgical history of ceremonies ceases to be of merely academic interest, and acquires considerable importance. To ascertain dispassionately the exact facts as to the origin, development, purpose, and meaning of a ceremony is the first step needed for a calm and judicial decision upon its claim to be recognised, in any revision of our services, as a wise and helpful adjunct to divine worship.

Ceremonies cannot be rightly studied apart from the circumstances that gave rise to them, the theological ideas which have become associated with them, the impression which they generally produce upon the popular mind. Hooker tells us that they are "resemblances framed according to things spiritually understood, whereunto they serve as a hand to lead, and a way to direct[1]." That is to say, a really helpful ceremony is not merely the decent accessory to a public act, calculated vaguely to impress the mind with reverence, like the ceremonial of some civic or national celebration, but it is, or ought to be, *significant*, and so likely to teach and stir the hearts and minds of men.

But it must not be forgotten, that ceremonies cannot teach with the same sharpness of definition which is found in an accurate statement as to doctrine or devotion To be helpful they must correspond to what they are intended to signify, but that correspondence, from its very nature, must be liable to varying interpretations; and a ceremony which has been used for many centuries, and has been associated with widely different ideas, must be regarded in the light not only of *what it is now intended to suggest by those who adopt it*, but of the meaning and influence which it has had in the past, and which it is therefore likely to have on the *popular* mind in the present day. These considerations apply with special force to the ceremony of elevation.

[1] Hooker, *Eccl. Pol.* iv. 1. 3. See the Bishop of Oxford's *Visitation Charge*, 1906, pp 5—8.

The history of elevation is full of complicated issues. The ceremony itself is easily adapted to varied interpretations, and it has accordingly been adopted at different points in the service with different shades of significance. Lapse of time has also tended in some cases to obscure the original purpose, and the ceremony has come to be a stereotyped piece of ritual, vaguely significant of devotion, but lacking definiteness of intention.

Six distinct places can be pointed out at which, in one or other of the groups of Liturgies, this ceremony occurs. There are elevations of

(1) the gifts of the people at the Offertory.
(2) the Bread and Wine at the words "Qui pridie" and "Simili modo."
(3) the Bread and Wine immediately after the consecration of each element.
(4) the Bread and Wine together at the close of the Western Canon.
(5) the consecrated Bread before the communion of the people in Eastern Liturgies, accompanied by the words τὰ ἅγια τοῖς ἁγίοις.
(6) the consecrated Bread at the communion of the people in the Church of Rome, accompanied by the words *Ecce Agnus Dei, Ecce qui tollit peccata mundi.*

The object of this enquiry is to trace the origin, use, and meaning of each of these forms of elevation, and where needful to disentangle its earlier from its later purpose. The investigation is historical, and involves an appeal to the Liturgies of the East, the Sacramentaries and Missals of the West, and also to those early and mediæval authors who have written on matters of sacred ritual.

The act of elevation, that is of lifting up the Bread and Wine, set apart for consecration or already consecrated, may signify one of two distinct things.

(1) It may partake of the nature of the heave offering, as illustrated in the Peace Offering of the Jewish ritual[1]. The parts assigned to the priest in that offering were lifted up before the altar as "a declaration in action" that they belonged to God. It was a symbolical offering of certain parts of the victim to God, which were then taken back as a gift from God and consumed by the priest.

This view of the ceremony includes the presentation of gifts of all kinds to God for His service, whether of "alms and oblations" generally, or specially of the Bread and Wine for His blessing before Communion.

[1] Bona (*Rerum Liturg.* II. XIII. 2) quotes a curious perversion of the Chaldee Paraphrase on Ps lxxii 16, "Erit placenta tritici in capitibus sacerdotum," in support of this kind of elevation. The ultimate source of his erroneous statement about this Targum is the "Additions" of Paul of Burgos (1400 A.D.) to the *Postillæ* of Nicholas de Lyra.

It also includes the idea of a presentation to God of a memorial of the Sacrifice of our Blessed Lord, or, as it came in later days to be regarded, an act in which "the Priest did offer Christ for the quick and the dead, to have remission of pain or guilt" (Art. xxxi.).

This is the *God-ward* aspect of elevation.

(2) It may be employed for the more usual purpose of displaying to the people the elements now prepared and consecrated for their use. But here a yet more marked divergence of view appears, for this form of elevation has denoted very distinct theological ideas.

(*a*) Sometimes the simpler idea has prevailed of presenting to the people the gifts as they were brought forward for their act of communion. Thus regarded the ceremony was both an invitation and a warning— an invitation to draw near, a warning that holy things are only for holy men. The exhibiting of the sacred symbols of redemption would naturally serve to stir dull minds to a more vivid remembrance of their Redeemer, and would thus call forth more intense devotion.

(*b*) But this earlier use of the ceremony acquired a different meaning, when the belief in an objective presence was developed by the Schoolmen into the doctrine of a corporal and local presence, and issued in the dogma of Transubstantiation. The devout worship of our Lord's spiritual presence in the Sacrament came to be directed towards His very Body and Blood as present in substance under the form of Bread and Wine, and the ceremony of Elevation became a signal that, the consecration being now complete, distinct reverence was at once due to the consecrated species. It will appear that this doctrine, thus sharply defined in A.D. 1215, produced a great crisis in the development of Eucharistic ceremonial in the West.

This is the *man-ward* aspect of elevation.

These main lines of divergent thought will appear again and again in this enquiry, and must constantly be borne in mind. Other subsidiary shades of meaning will also appear, but they can generally be differentiated by means of these fundamental distinctions

CHAPTER I.

EASTERN LITURGIES.

IT is natural to begin by examining the Liturgies of the East. The ceremony of elevation appears in them for the most part at one definite point of the service, not at several points as in the ritual of the West. Its meaning moreover is less complex, the enquiry being disturbed by fewer cross-currents of doctrine and variations of usage. Our first enquiry will therefore be this—Where did elevation occur, and what did it mean, in the Eastern Liturgies?

(1) *Elevation at the Offertory.*

The offering of the gifts, and specially of the Bread and Wine destined for Eucharistic use, was a marked feature in the Oriental rite. As this offering eventually came to be accompanied by a distinct act of elevation in the West, it might well be expected that the same ceremony would accompany it in the East. But there is no trace of such a ceremony in this connexion in the *public* part of the services, though it is found as a later development in a *Prothesis* of the Liturgy of St Chrysostom of about the 14th century, and is referred to by Cardinal Humbert in the 11th century[1]. The offering of the unconsecrated gifts once occupied a marked position at the commencement of the Mass of the faithful before the Anaphora. It is probably referred to by St Clement of Rome (I *Epist.* c. xliv.) where he speaks of the sin of casting off those who "without blame and holily offer the gifts[2]": and several early writers make it clear that the offerings of the people, including the Bread and Wine afterwards used at the Communion, were placed upon the Holy Table by one of the ministers and so offered on behalf of the people[3]. In other words there was a lay oblation

---

[1] Brightman, p 548, λαβὼν τὸν ἄρτον ὑψοῖ αὐτὸν ἀκροδάκτυλον (*Lit. St Chrys.*). The *Prothesis* is really the second part of the Offertory (viz the preparation of the elements after the offering of the people), put out of its place at the commencement of the service and performed in a side chapel. This *Prothesis-elevation* is alluded to by Cardinal Humbert (c. 1050, *Contra Græcorum Calumnias*), "Porro in præfatis sanctis ecclesiis cum ipsa sancta patina *sanctam anaphoram*, i.e. oblationem, *exaltant.*" He is speaking of the ritual preparation of the elements with the λόγχη in the *Prothesis*. Brightman, p. 541.

[2] Bishop Lightfoot raises the question in what sense the presbyter might be said to "offer the gifts." After quoting various passages, he adds, "They led the prayers and thanksgivings of the congregation, they presented the alms and contributions to God, and asked His blessing upon them in the name of the whole body. Hence Clement is careful to insist (§ 40) that these offerings should be made at the right time, and in the right place, and by the right people." Bp Lightfoot, *Clement of Rome*, Pt I. Vol. ii. p. 135.

[3] *Const. Apost* ii. 25, 27, 34, 53. Ambrosiaster, *Quæst. ex Vet.*

followed by a more formal ministerial oblation of gifts devoted to the service of God[1].

This oblation of the unconsecrated gifts is clearly recognised in the Greek Liturgies at the "Great Entrance," when the offerings, already prepared in the Chapel of the *Prothesis*, are carried by the deacons and placed upon the Holy Table. This action is expressed by the word προτιθέναι, and the offerings thus set forth are τὰ προκείμενα δῶρα. Thus in the Liturgy of St Mark we find Σοὶ ἐκ τῶν σῶν δώρων προεθήκαμεν ἐνώπιόν σου: and in the Liturgy of St Basil, ὑπομνήματα τοῦ σωτηρίου αὐτοῦ πάθους ταῦτα ἃ προτεθείκαμεν[2].

Test. 46, Migne, *P.L* xxxv. 2246. St Aug *Enarr. in Psalm.* 129, § 7, ib. xxxvii. p. 1701. St Cæsarius, *Serm.* 66, § 2. John the Deacon, *Life of Gregory the Great*, ii. § 41, Migne, *P.L.* lxxv. 103.

[1] Theodoret relates how the Emperor Valens was allowed to enter εἰς τὸν θεῖον νεών, and after receiving instruction from St Basil, to offer personally the wonted gifts—καὶ τῷ θυσιαστηρίῳ τὰ εἰωθότα προσενήνοχε δῶρα. *Eccles. Hist.* iv. 16, Migne, *P.G.* lxxxii. 1161. Cf. Greg. Naz. *Orat* xliii. 52, ib. xxxvi. 564. The 2nd Canon of the Council of Ancyra (A.D. 314) describes part of the "sacred service" of the deacon as ἄρτον ἢ ποτήριον ἀναφέρειν. Mansi ii. p 513. On these grounds Mr Brightman thus reconstructs the Offertory of the Pontic Liturgy (pp. 522, 525 n.),

ὁ λαὸς προσφέρει τὰ δῶρα,
οἱ διάκονοι ἀναφέρουσι.

[2] Brightman, *Eastern Lit.* pp. 122, 133, 327, 381. Cf. Cyril Jer. *Mystag.* v. c. 7, 19. *Const. Apost.* viii c. 12. The language employed suggests that the setting the shewbread in order was borne in mind. See Ex. xl. 4, 23, Levit. xxiv. 8, Heb. עָרַךְ, LXX. προτιθέναι. Cf. Ex. xxxix. 36, where the LXX. τοὺς ἄρτους τοὺς προκειμένους (*v. l.* τῆς προθέσεως) stands for the Hebrew לֶחֶם הַפָּנִים. Cf. Levit xxiv. 7

But although there is early evidence of such an offering, and although the Liturgies direct with elaborate exactness all the ritual details of the "Great Entrance," yet no public ceremony of elevation seems to be enjoined, beyond what was necessary for the carrying out of the simple order—ἀποτίθησι μὲν ὁ ἱερεὺς τὸ ἅγιον ποτήριον ἐν τῇ ἁγίᾳ τραπέζῃ κ.τ λ.[1] There was a πρόθεσις, but no ὕψωσις.

The elevation at the Offertory of the Western service will come before us at a later period. In the Eastern Church we have found no trace (outside the *prothesis*) of any distinct direction to lift up the gifts at this point in order to signify their presentation to God, though of that presentation itself there can be no doubt.

(2) *Elevation at the Words of Institution.*

The next point at which we meet the ceremony of elevation is at the opening words of both parts of the Words of Institution. In the Latin Canon the Bread was (generally) elevated at "Qui pridie," and the Cup at "Simili modo" In Eastern Liturgies the actual traces of the ceremony at this part of the service are few, but the point of interest is that we find the opening words of the Institution so developed in the East as to illustrate the act of elevation in the West.

[1] *Lit. of St Chrys.* Brightman, p. 379.

EASTERN LITURGIES

It will be borne in mind that a great variety of opinion has existed as to what constitutes the actual formula of consecration. The Latin Church identifies them with the recital of the Institution, the Greek Church with the *Epiclesis*, or prayer for the Holy Ghost to sanctify the elements, while an early tradition (accepted by Gregory the Great, and repeated by the ritualist Amalarius in the 9th century) records that the Apostles at the consecration of the Eucharist used only the Lord's Prayer[1]. It is probable that the most certain conclusion to be drawn is that the earliest Christians laid no special stress upon any particular form of words *as essential to consecration*, and that the thought of *thanksgiving* was more predominant in their minds than that of *consecration*, the presence of our Lord to bestow His blessing being associated with the whole act of worship, rather than with a particular point of the service or with any one particular form of words.

That there was a belief in what is rightly called "consecration" is clear, but the words used by Justin Martyr and Clement Alex. (εὐχαριστηθεὶς ἄρτος, ὕδωρ

[1] Gregory found the Consecration separated from our Lord's own prayer, and he comments on the inconsistency of it. "Et valde mihi inconveniens visum est ut precem quam scholasticus composuerat super Oblationem diceremus, et ipsam traditionem quam Redemptor noster composuerat super ejus Corpus et Sanguinem non diceremus." Greg. Magn. *Opera*, Migne, *P.L.* lxxvii. c. 956 f. Cf. Drury, *Two Studies* (Nisbet), pp. 10 f.

ψιλὸν εὐχαριστοῦσιν) show that the central thought, which involved consecration, was that of blessing or thanking God for His gift of heavenly food in Jesus Christ. This is illustrated by the early use (e.g. in the *Didache*, Ignatius, and Justin Martyr[1]) of the word *Eucharistia* to denote the "Breaking of Bread."

Justin Martyr's words δι' εὐχῆς λόγου τοῦ παρ' αὐτοῦ seem to point clearly to a tradition of some form of words having been given by our Lord, although what they were we cannot now certainly decide. The tradition that the Apostles used the Lord's Prayer alone would suitably interpret his words, and the recital of the Institution may have originally been used *not as a prayer*, but as a commemorative and descriptive act, uttered in grateful acknowledgment of God's greatest gift. The recital of the Institution and the Lord's Prayer are common to nearly all Liturgies[2], and this fact points to the primitive origin of both. Gregory's words do not exclude this explanation, for in speaking of "*that very prayer*[3]," he does not exclude other words of commemoration or thanksgiving.

[1] *Didache*, c. 9, 10. Ignatius, *ad Smyrn.* c. 7, 8; *ad Philadelph.* c. 4. Justin M. *Apol.* i. c. 96. The passage in the *Didache* is full of the thought of thanksgiving.

[2] The "Institution" is not named in the earliest writers on the Eucharist, nor in St Cyril Jer. It is absent from the Nestorian Lit. of SS. Adæus and Maris which is of early date. The few cases in which the Lord's Prayer is absent are given in Drury, *Two Studies*, p 12.

[3] "ipsam traditionem (*sic*) quam Redemptor noster composuerat." Greg. Magn. *loc. cit.* In Hermann's *Consultatio* the prayer of con-

There is possibly a trace of this bare recital of the narrative, apart from prayer, in the Ethiopic and Nestorian Liturgies, no words of address to God *being inserted in it*, although it forms part of an act of thanksgiving[1]. In the Ethiopic, as in other Liturgies, the recital of the Institution is made the basis of the prayer of *Epiclesis* (Μεμνημένοι οὖν κ.τ.λ.[2]), and this appears to be the most natural relation of that recital to the other parts of the consecration. We say what our Lord said and do what He did, and make it our ground of access and our plea for the bestowal of spiritual blessings. Early as some form of *Epiclesis* must have been, from its widespread use, it would seem to have been a subsequent development out of the recital of what our Lord said and did[3].

secration consists simply of the Words of Institution and the Lord's Prayer.

[1] Brightman, pp. 190, 285 In the Nestorian rite however the Institution (as Mr Brightman points out) is "obviously incoherent with the context"

[2] Brightman, pp. 52, 87, &c.

[3] In the *Euchologion* of Serapion, Bishop of Thmuis and friend of St Athanasius, it is noticeable that the "Holy Word" is invoked upon the elements in place of the Holy Spirit as in the normal *Epiclesis*. This early form recalls the words of St Paul in 1 Tim. iv. 5, where he says that "every creature of God is good," "if it be received with thanksgiving, for it is *sanctified by the word of God and prayer*." The reference to the sanctification of our common food by sacred word and intercession at least suggests the early use of some such formula at the Supper of the Lord. The words of Serapion's Eucharistic prayer may be a connecting link between the general idea of the consecration of food which is expressed in 1 Tim. iv, and the more fully developed *Epiclesis* of the Eastern Church.

This desire to reproduce our Lord's own form appears in writers such as St Chrysostom. But in later times more stress is laid on the *ipsissima verba* than upon the whole action, and this developed into localising the consecration, in the West, in the actual words, "This is my Body," "This is my Blood."

St Chrysostom, after saying that the oblation is the same whosoever may offer it, and that the consecration is not man's, but His who consecrated at the first, adds, ὥσπερ γὰρ τὰ ῥήματα, ἅπερ ὁ θεὸς ἐφθέγξατο, τὰ αὐτά ἐστιν, ἅπερ ὁ ἱερεὺς καὶ νῦν λέγει, οὕτω καὶ ἡ προσφορὰ ἡ αὐτή ἐστι[1].

In another passage he speaks of the permanent force of the words "Be fruitful and multiply," and says οὕτω καὶ ἡ φωνὴ αὕτη ἅπαξ λεχθεῖσα καθ' ἑκάστην τράπεζαν ἐν ταῖς ἐκκλησίαις ἐξ ἐκείνου μέχρι σήμερον καὶ μέχρι τῆς αὐτοῦ παρουσίας τὴν θυσίαν ἀπαρτισμένην ἐργάζεται[2].

Yet this natural desire and intention to base the

---

[1] St Chrys. *in* 2 *Tim.* ii. 4, Migne, *P.G.* lxii. p. 612.

[2] *De Prodit. Judæ*, i. 6, Migne, xlix. p. 380. Martene quotes from a Cistercian Sacramentary, "Christi ergo virtute et verbis iste panis et calix ab initio consecratus est. Christi virtute et verbis semper consecratur et consecrabitur". and again Gerbert quotes from a *Missale Monasterii Ursinensis* of the 15th century, where stress is laid on *the intention* to consecrate by using the very words of Christ. "*Intentio ante consecrationem* intendo nunc consecrare...per verba ejusdem salvatoris nostri Jesus Christi, *Qui Pridie &c.*" Martene, *Voy. Lit.* (A.D. 1724), p. 107. Gerbert, i. Disq. iv. 29, p. 360. See also Amalar. *De Off. Eccles.* 1. 15, Gerbert, i. p. 361, Hittorp. P. ii. p. 544 f.

whole act of the Eucharist upon the record of the original words and action of our Lord did not prevent distinct additions being made to the recorded words of Institution. This is evident from the form of recital found in the vast majority of the Liturgies. Only a few confine them to the written words of the New Testament. Thus the Ethiopic and Nestorian Liturgies contain no enlargement of the original narrative. The former even errs by defect, for the word "brake" is omitted, and the latter has a form not unlike that in the Mozarabic rite and in the Anglican Communion Office.

St Basil explains these additions as derived from early unwritten testimony as to our Lord's manner of instituting the Eucharist. On a matter of such central interest it is likely that tradition would preserve certain additional details, and he justifies the enlargement of the recital on these grounds.

Οὐ γὰρ δὴ τούτοις ἀρκούμεθα ὧν ὁ ἀπόστολος ἢ τὸ εὐαγγέλιον ἐπεμνήσθη, ἀλλὰ καὶ προλέγομεν καὶ ἐπιλέγομεν ἕτερα,...ὡς μεγάλην ἔχοντα πρὸς τὸ μυστήριον τὴν ἰσχύν, ἐκ τῆς ἀγράφου διδασκαλίας παραλαβόντες[1].

This implies the recital of the Institution as found in the Gospels, together with certain ἄγραφα or unwritten circumstances which St Basil believed to be authentic (Innocent III. and after him Gabriel Biel repeat the same opinion. See Gerbert, I. iv. 29)

[1] St Basil, *De Spir. Sanct.* xxvii. 66, Migne, *P.G.* xxxii. 188.

The account given by St Basil agrees with the phenomena of the Liturgies, where we find several such additions describing more particularly our Lord's actions at the Last Supper, some of which throw light upon our enquiry.

The most common addition is that which supplements the simple expression λαβὼν (τὸν) ἄρτον by such words as ταῖς ἁγίαις καὶ ἀμώμοις αὐτοῦ χερσί (*Apost. Constit.*), or ἐπὶ τῶν ἁγίων καὶ ἀχράντων καὶ ἀμώμων καὶ ἀθανάτων αὐτοῦ χειρῶν[1] (Syr. Lit. of St James). This addition is almost universal, and is represented in the words of the Western Missals *in sanctas et venerabiles manus*.

Again, the sacred records give the simple words εὐχαριστήσας or εὐλογήσας, but these are expanded in the Liturgies from another passage in our Lord's life. He is described as "looking up" (ἀναβλέψας) in the act of giving thanks, as in the Synoptists' account of the feeding of the five thousand (λαβὼν τοὺς πέντε ἄρτους ...ἀναβλέψας εἰς τὸν οὐρανὸν εὐλόγησεν καὶ κλάσας ἔδωκεν, St Matt. xiv. 19). Sometimes the phrase is exactly that found in the Synoptic account of that miracle—ἀναβλέψας εἰς τὸν οὐρανόν (Syr. Lit. of St James). sometimes the idea is expanded, and a direct address to God is introduced into the simple

[1] St Cyril Jer. uses the phrase ἐπὶ τῶν ἀχράντων αὐτοῦ χειρῶν, but not in this connexion He is speaking of our Lord's crucifixion and of the nails driven into His spotless hands and feet. *Mystag.* ii. 5, Migne, *P.G.* xxxiii. 1081 A.

recital, by such words as πρὸς σὲ τὸν θεὸν καὶ πατέρα. This too is very general and finds a place in the Western Missals—*elevatis oculis in cœlum ad Te Deum Patrem suum omnipotentem.* These additions do little more than enrich the narrative, but in a few cases a distinctly doctrinal shade of meaning appears in the significant words—καὶ ἀναδείξας σοὶ τῷ Θεῷ καὶ Πατρί (Syr. Lit. of St James, Syr. Jacobites) The same words appear in one form of the Byzantine Liturgy of St Basil (ninth or tenth century), though absent from the earlier ninth century form of St Basil, and wholly from that of St Chrysostom, including the modern rite[1].

Of these later interpolations, one (as we have seen) is evidently borrowed from another recorded act of blessing in which the additional words occur[2]. It was not unnatural thus to generalise, by assuming this to have been our Lord's custom in all such acts, even though no tradition actually named it. The other expansions have no support from the New Testament narratives.

The addition of the word ἁγιάσας in several Liturgies is interesting as showing that consecration

[1] Brightman, pp. 52, 87, 327. See p. 308 and 327 note *a*.

[2] Gerbert (1. Disq. IV. § 29) remarks that such additions are not found in the Gospel accounts of the Institution, adding, "aliunde autem ex omnibus quatuor evangelistis constat Christum gratias acturum oculos in cœlum sustulisse." It is used in St John (xvii. 1) of our Lord's attitude *in prayer.*

or sanctification was regarded as one main purpose of this recital. God was thanked, and thereby the gifts were sanctified. St Paul uses ἁγιάζειν in 1 Tim. iv. 5 of the sanctification of our common food διὰ λόγου Θεοῦ καὶ ἐντεύξεως, and this idea was naturally transferred with a nobler meaning to the Eucharist[1]. The passage, thus applied, may account for the importance attached to the recital of the Gospel narrative as the λόγος Θεοῦ, when the inspired utterances of Apostles and Prophets, as described in the *Didache*, had died away[2]. While they lived they may have supplied, when present, the requisite "Word of God"; but afterwards some part of *the written word* would be adopted.

Yet when we seek for evidence of any ceremonial acts with which the celebrant was to accompany the recital of the Institution, we find that in the Eastern Church they are very scanty. It is so in the case of Elevation. In the Western Church this expansion of the recital expressed itself in action more freely, but in the Eastern the rubrics directing such action are very few indeed.

---

[1] Origen and St Gregory of Nyssa expressly say that the elements are consecrated "by the Word of God and prayer." Origen *in Matt.* xi. 14, Migne, *P.G.* xiii. p. 949. St Greg. Nyss. *Oratio Catech.*, c. 37, Migne, xlv. p. 97.

[2] τοῖς δὲ προφήταις ἐπιτρέπετε εὐχαριστεῖν ὅσα θέλουσιν. *Didache*, c. x. Cf εὐχὰς ὁμοίως καὶ εὐχαριστίας, ὅση δύναμις αὐτῷ, ἀναπέμπει. Just. Martyr, *Apol.* i. 67.

The most notable absence of corresponding ceremonial is that of "fraction" at the words of Institution. This action is most natural as reproducing that of our Lord Himself. The "taking," "breaking," and "giving" are the only three manual acts named, yet the "breaking" is absent from most of the Greek Liturgies, and from at least one (the Ethiopic) even the word κλάσας has disappeared. It is found in other Egyptian Liturgies, namely those of the Coptic and Abyssinian Jacobites.

This earlier and really primitive fraction (κλάσις) gave place both in East and West to the ceremonial dividing for distribution (μελισμός), which followed consecration. The primitive ceremony of breaking the bread was restored in the Anglican rite in 1662.

It is difficult to assign exact dates to particular expressions found in the Liturgies, but we are in some measure able to supplement their evidence from writers whose date is known, and much has been done by Mr Hammond and Mr Brightman in reconstructing the ancient services by this means.

Two words are used by early writers, ἀναδείκνυμι (or ἀποδείκνυμι) and ὑποδείκνυμι, both of which are found in liturgical contexts. Ὑποδείκνυμι means "to show forth," "to make a display of," and fitly denotes that "showing to the people" which took place in all Eastern Liturgies after consecration. Its use in relation to our subject will be discussed later on, but the former word (ἀναδείκνυμι) claims immediate attention.

The meaning of ἀναδείκνυμι and of the substantive ἀνάδειξις is more complex. The verb cannot be pressed to mean "lift up and show," it simply means to "exhibit" or "display." This use of the word is found in several Liturgies, where the words ἀναδείξας τῷ Θεῷ κ.τ.λ. have been added to the narrative of the Evangelists.

Again, in a Byzantine writer of the 6th century, St Eutychius, and in a passage apparently liturgical, the full expression ἀναδείξας τῷ Θεῷ καὶ Πατρί is used of the Cup, while the word ἀνέδειξε is used absolutely of the Bread[1].

But the word has also certain secondary meanings. In the Liturgy of the *Apost. Constit.* it is almost equivalent to ποιεῖν—τὸν κοσμοπολίτην ἄνθρωπον ἐν αὐτῷ (κόσμῳ) ἐποίησας, κόσμου κόσμον ἀναδείξας. Again, τοὺς ἐν κατηχήσει παίδευσον καὶ τῆς μυήσεως ἀξίους ἀνάδειξον. In the Byzantine Liturgy of the Praesanctified we find μέλη τίμια τοῦ Χριστοῦ σου ἀνάδειξον (αὐτούς)[2]. The word may here mean "show to be," "exhibit as being," but its significance closely assimilates to the simple "make."

---

[1] Εὐχαριστήσας ἀνέδειξε καὶ ἔκλασεν . κεράσας καὶ εὐχαριστήσας καὶ ἀναδείξας τῷ Θεῷ καὶ Πατρί. Eutych *de Paschate*, Migne, *P.G.* lxxxvi (2), 2393 B

[2] Brightman, pp. 16, 26, 347. The verb ἀποφαίνειν has the same meaning, and is found often in Cyril-Al., as well as in the Lit. of *Apost. Const. Ib.* p. 8.

A still more special shade of meaning attaches to it when used in the *Epiclesis* of the Liturgy of St Basil (9th century). Εὐλογῆσαι αὐτὰ καὶ ἁγιάσαι καὶ ἀναδεῖξαι τὸν μὲν ἄρτον τοῦτον αὐτὸ τὸ τίμιον σῶμα τοῦ κυρίου[1]. Here ἀναδεῖξαι describes the result of the *Epiclesis*, which the Eastern Church regarded as the actual words of consecration This connexion between ἀναδείκνυμι and the ἐπίκλησις is further illustrated by a passage in St Basil, which will shortly be considered.

The word is thus seen to be used *in two senses,* both of which are closely related to the consecration. It may denote the action of our Lord, which came to be regarded as a showing to the Father of the gifts of bread and wine, or the resultant act of blessing by virtue of which the gifts are declared to be (as in the Latin Canon, " ut nobis Corpus et Sanguis fiat ") the Body and Blood of Christ. This use of the word ἀναδείκνυμι has led to its being generally taken to signify " *to consecrate.*"

We proceed to consider the earliest passage in which we have found ἀνάδειξις applied to the Eucharist. St Basil writes,

Τὰ τῆς ἐπικλήσεως ῥήματα ἐπὶ τῇ ἀναδείξει τοῦ ἄρτου τῆς εὐχαριστίας καὶ τοῦ ποτηρίου τῆς εὐλογίας, τίς τῶν ἁγίων ἐγγράφως ἡμῖν καταλέλοιπεν[2],

Here we have at the close of the 4th century the

---

[1] *Ib* p. 329. So ἀποφαίνειν in the *Epiclesis* of the *Apost. Const.* ὅπως ἀποφήνῃ τὸν ἄρτον τοῦτον σῶμα τοῦ χριστοῦ σου *Ib* p. 21.

[2] St Basil, *de Spiritu Sancto,* xxvii. 66, Migne, *P.G.* xxxii. 188.

words ἐπίκλησις and ἀνάδειξις used in connexion with the Eucharist, and the occurrence of the two words in the same context is full of interest. St Basil expresses a doubt as to whether any record of the original words of ἐπίκλησις existed in his day, and refers to them as occurring at the ἀνάδειξις of the Bread and Wine.

In later days Cardinal Bellarmine used this passage in support of the early origin of elevation for the purpose of showing the elements to the people for adoration. He gives the following account of St Basil's words:

Verba invocationis cum ostenditur panis Eucharistiæ, quis sanctorum in scripto nobis reliquit? Hinc enim habemus morem fuisse in Ecclesiâ veteri, ut post consecrationem ostenderetur populo Eucharistia, quod etiam nunc fieri videmus; et conceptis verbis invocaretur, quæ verba quidam suspicatur fuisse, *Kyrieeleison.* Sed certe ex invocatione manifeste colligitur veritas Christi in Eucharistia. neque enim panem invocare possumus quantumlibet significet, vel representet Corpus Christi[1].

Bellarmine here interprets St Basil's " words of invocation" to be those in which *the people invoke the Eucharist when it is shown to them.* For such an interpretation there appears to be no warrant whatever. The words ἀνάδειξις, ἀναδείκνυμι do not appear to denote an exhibition to the people, nor does ἐπίκλησις ever mean an invocation of the elements. It is moreover most improbable that the words refer to the Greek elevation after the Lord's Prayer, since the words

[1] Bellarmine, *De Eucharist.*, L. ii. c 15.

ἐπίκλησις and ἀναδείκνυμι belong to an earlier point in the service. Lastly, the Greek elevation was not to evoke adoration, and such an interpretation reads into the words the theological ideas and liturgical ceremonies of a much later date.

Whether the word ἐπίκλησις is used by St Basil in its technical sense may be doubtful, but it certainly refers to some words of appeal to God of which it was desirable to have an authentic record, if it could be obtained. These considerations lead to the conclusion that the reference in St Basil is to some words closely associated with the consecration, and not with the subsequent displaying of the consecrated gifts to the people. To the latter belongs the word ὑποδείξας, as in the passage from Dionysius Areopagita quoted below, but ἀναδείξας has never such a significance.

Bingham's translation of St Basil's words thus appears to be perfectly justified:—"Which of the saints has left us in writing the words of the invocation or prayer, *wherewith the Eucharist is consecrated*[1]?" Bishop J. Wordsworth and Mr Brightman both adopt the same conclusion, and interpret ἀνάδειξις as meaning "consecration." The gifts presented to God for His service were thus declared to be, were exhibited as being, in the sense of the Founder's own words, the Body and the Blood of Christ.

[1] Bingham, *Chr. Ant.* xv. 5, § 4. Bp Wordsworth, *Holy Com.* p. 98. Brightman, p. 594.

Ἀναδείκνυμι and ἀνάδειξις may therefore be taken to refer to the consecration. Originally they may have been connected with the element of thanksgiving which was so dominant an idea in primitive Eucharists. The devout purpose of thanking God for His manifold gifts was symbolised by the offerings then presented before Him. In course of time, our Lord's action in taking bread, breaking, and giving thanks was interpreted to be an act of dedication to God, a grateful commemoration of His manifold blessings, made with His own gifts to man. On the other hand, the divine answer to this Eucharistic acknowledgment was the blessing of these gifts to sacred use, their sanctification or consecration, so that they were no longer common food but declared to be, according to the meaning placed on them by our Lord Himself, His own Body and Blood.

We might have expected that this development of the idea of an Eucharistic surrender of our gifts to God, in acknowledgment of His best and greatest gift to us, would have been accompanied by some corresponding extension of the manual acts It was so in the West, but in the East the evidence of it is scanty and of a later date. The simple act of taking the bread into the hands, while giving thanks, was all that the Gospel narratives seemed to imply, and that was enough.

Thus in the Greek Liturgy of St James the simple

direction is given εἶτα ὁ ἱερεὺς τῇ χειρὶ τὸν ἄρτον κατασχὼν λέγει, λαβὼν τὸν ἄρτον κ.τ.λ.[1]

In a writer of the 7th or 8th century we find an account of an Eucharistic service which implies a more definite ceremony. James of Edessa, in a letter to Thomas the Presbyter, speaks of the celebrant as doing, in the action which he describes, what our Lord did at the original institution. He says: "We hold the peristo of the bread and show it to God the Father, as the Son also showed it, and say, 'When He had given thanks He blessed,' and the rest[2]." This was simply to translate into action the words of the recital as found in the Liturgies of St Basil and St James and of the Syrian Jacobites (see p. 19). No actual elevation is named, but in the Liturgy of the Coptic Jacobites there is a late rubric expressly directing a manual act of elevation at this place. "[*He shall take the bread upon his hands saying*] TOOK BREAD upon His holy spotless and undefiled and lifegiving hands, [*he shall raise his hands with the bread while his gaze is directed upwards and shall say*] LOOKED UP TO HEAVEN, etc." This is the only place (so far as this enquiry has gone) where elevation is expressly directed, and the rubrics are taken from the Liturgies and a Deacon's Manual published at Cairo in 1887[3].

[1] Brightman, p. 51.
[2] *Ib.* p. 493.
[3] Brightman, p. 176. See p. 112, n. 2.

This fact that the Eastern Church did not clearly mark any oblation of the Bread and Wine before the recital of the Institution, as the Western Church did, may arise from their placing the act of consecration, not in "the recital," but in the *Epiclesis*.

Now the *Epiclesis* is preceded in all Eastern Liturgies by a distinct oblation. The Bread and Wine are, immediately after the words of institution, offered to God as an "unbloody sacrifice," and the prayer for the descent of the Holy Spirit follows. If we are right in this suggestion, the Eastern Church makes this offering *after* the words of Institution, while the Western Church makes it *before* them[1], because of the different place assigned in each case to the act of consecration. What is noteworthy is that in both cases *an act of oblation immediately precedes consecration*, though unaccompanied by any definite act of elevation in the Eastern Church.

We have found no certain evidence of an early date that any corresponding ceremonial, beyond the simple acts described in the Gospels, was practised immediately before or at the consecration in the Eastern Church. The idea of presentation to God was there, but we cannot find that it found expression in any outward sign. It must, it is true, be

---

[1] Cf the "Quam oblationem" of the Western Canon immediately before the Words of Institution. Similar words of oblation to those used in the Greek Liturgies also follow the Institution in the Western Canon, but without any explicit form of *Epiclesis*.

remembered that in the earlier forms of the Liturgies rubrical directions are few, and that traditional ceremonies may have existed, even when not expressed in any formal rubric. But it is unlikely that so significant an act as that of elevation, in a God-ward sense, could have been generally practised without finding mention either in the Liturgies themselves or in contemporary liturgical writers It is at least possible, if not probable, that the express direction to elevate in the Coptic Liturgy, at the words "looked up to heaven," may be a later interpolation of the undoubted ceremony of elevation at the "Qui pridie" of the Western rite, just as the later elevation immediately after consecration is found in some Eastern services, though clearly foreign to the universal Eastern use.

We have now reviewed the evidence bearing on Eastern Liturgies as to elevation before consecration. Of elevation for the purpose of showing to the people there is no trace, and although the thought of presentation to God is present both at the offertory, and in the eucharistic recital of the Institution, yet there is but little distinct testimony that a corresponding act of lifting up accompanied the words used by the celebrant. The placing of the gifts upon the Holy Table, and the taking of the bread and wine into the hands of the celebrant, were regarded as sufficiently significant of this eucharistic idea, which is illustrated by the tendency in most Liturgies to expand, and in a few to interpret, the narrative of the Evangelists and of St Paul. The Western mind tended to translate this idea more definitely into action.

It is further to be noted that the distinctly sacrificial phrases of these Liturgies do not appear to have suggested this ceremony in its God-ward meaning. For example, the prayer of *Epiclesis* always contains such words as προσφέρομέν σοι δέσποτα τὴν φοβερὰν ταύτην καὶ ἀναίμακτον θυσίαν, but no trace of any corresponding ceremony is found, although elevation, if taken in its sacrificial meaning, would here be most appropriate to the words used. In fact elevation does not seem to have been employed, to any marked extent, for this particular purpose in the early Eastern Liturgies.

(3) *Elevation at the words* τὰ ἅγια τοῖς ἁγίοις.

The one clearly marked elevation in the East always follows the Consecration and the Lord's Prayer, and introduces the Communion of the people. Writers of the Roman Church point out the distinction of time between the Churches of the East and West, while they confuse the distinction of purpose. Bona thus distinguishes the times of elevation, "Latini peractâ consecratione, Græci paulo ante communionem[1]." Sala, following Renaudot, says, " Non statim post conse-

[1] Bona, *Rer. Lit* L. II xiii. 2.

crationem, ut Latini, sed post Orationem Dominicalem (*sic*) seu paulo ante communionem, ut Græci[1]." But when Bona adds that the purpose of the Greek elevation was "ut a populo adoretur," he introduces an interpretation of the ceremony of elevation which is of much later origin and is peculiar to one form of Western theology.

The Eastern elevation is always found in close relation to the words, universally found at this point of the Eastern rite, τὰ ἅγια τοῖς ἁγίοις. On the other hand the words are not always accompanied by the ceremony, and are certainly of earlier date, the act of elevation having been added to enforce the message which the words conveyed.

It is therefore an important part of our enquiry to ascertain the meaning of the words τὰ ἅγια κ.τ.λ., and especially that which they generally bore when the act of elevation was adopted. Whatever may have been the original significance of the words, it is their accepted significance at the time when elevation arose, that will be our safest guide to its true purpose. Now, the generally accepted interpretation of τὰ ἅγια τοῖς ἁγίοις from the end of the 4th century admits of little, if any, doubt.

From the time of St Cyril of Jerusalem these words were taken to be, on the one hand, a public intimation to devout communicants that "the gifts"

[1] *Ib.* note 1. Renaudot, 1. p. 265.

were prepared for reception, and on the other hand a solemn warning against a profane use of holy things.

In this sense they seem to echo the divine appeal ἅγιοι ἔσεσθε ὅτι ἐγὼ ἅγιος, words which are found in the Syrian Lit. of St James in a prayer for sanctification (ἁγίασον ἡμᾶς) immediately following the elevation. They also enforce our Lord's own warning μὴ δότε τὸ ἅγιον τοῖς κυσί[1]. A prayer for holiness is generally found at this part of the service, the significance of which is that the special preparation of gifts should be followed by a special preparation of those for whom they were prepared. This feature is more clearly marked in Eastern Liturgies than in Western, a defect which the compilers of the "Order of Communion" in 1548 undoubtedly sought to remedy. In supplying that new Order they followed the general structure of the Eastern service, placing it after the Canon, so that it might serve as a preparation for the restored communion of the people. It continued to hold the same position in 1549. It is fair to surmise that in this suggestive sequence Cranmer was following, as we know he did, the guidance of early models. The purpose is obvious, and it illustrates the force of these words. The bread and wine become after consecration

---

[1] This warning is adopted in the *Didache* before reception, but with reference to the need of Baptism. "Let no one eat or drink of your Eucharist if he is not baptised in the name of the Lord, for it was of this the Lord said, 'Give not that which is holy to dogs.'" c. ix.

holy things,—*holy* also must be the persons who receive them. The fulness of the divine order demands that the sanctification of the people as well as the consecration of the elements must precede communion—Τὰ ἅγια τοῖς ἁγίοις.

The evidence external to the Liturgies themselves is wholly in favour of this interpretation, which is adopted in writers of different countries and of successive centuries. The earliest reference to this liturgical formula is given by St Cyril of Jerusalem in the 4th century.

Μετὰ ταῦτα λέγει ὁ ἱερεύς, τὰ ἅγια τοῖς ἁγίοις. ἅγια τὰ προκείμενα, ἐπιφοίτησιν δεξάμενα ἁγίου πνεύματος· ἅγιοι καὶ ὑμεῖς πνεύματος ἁγίου καταξιωθέντες. τὰ ἅγια οὖν τοῖς ἁγίοις κατάλληλα[1].

St Chrysostom is equally clear. In his comments on St Matt. vii. 6 he says:

Καὶ παρ' ἡμῶν αἰτεῖ [ὁ Χριστὸς] πιεῖν οὐχ ὕδωρ ἀλλ' ἁγιωσύνην, τὰ γὰρ ἅγια τοῖς ἁγίοις δίδωσιν.

In another passage, on the Epistle to the Hebrews, St Chrysostom is even more explicit. In the church, he says, there are healthy sheep and diseased (ὑγιεινά, κεκακωμένα), and by uttering the words τὰ ἅγια τοῖς ἁγίοις (τῆς κραυγῆς ταύτης φρικωδεστάτης), the priest

---

[1] St Cyril-Jer. *Mystagog.* v. c. xix., Migne, *P.G.* xxxiii. 1124. Cyril goes on to give the people's response, εἷς ἅγιος κ.τ.λ., and adds this comment, ἀληθῶς γὰρ εἷς ἅγιος, φύσει ἅγιος· ἡμεῖς δὲ καὶ ἅγιοι κ.τ.λ.

proclaims this distinction, "lifting up his hand on high like a herald." He adds:

Ὅταν γὰρ εἴπῃ 'τὰ ἅγια τοῖς ἁγίοις,' τοῦτο λέγει, Εἴ τις οὐκ ἔστιν ἅγιος μὴ προσίτω[1].

Passing from the 4th to the 5th century we find the same meaning unfolded by St Cyril of Alexandria[2] in a passage on St John xx.

Τοιγάρ τοι καὶ τοῖς μετασχεῖν ἐθέλουσιν εὐλογίας τῆς μυστικῆς οἱ τῶν θείων μυστηρίων προσφωνοῦσι λειτουργοὶ, τὰ ἅγια τοῖς ἁγίοις, πρεπωδεστάτην εἶναι διδάσκοντες τῶν ἁγίων τὴν μέθεξιν τοῖς ἡγιασμένοις ἐν πνεύματι.

In the 6th century we have the witness of a Syrian writer, Cyril of Scythopolis, who describes the exhibiting (ὑποδεικνύων) of the "mystery" to the people accompanied by the loud utterance of the words τὰ ἅγια κ.τ.λ., and then goes on to say:

Τὰ γὰρ ἅγια ταῦτα οὐχὶ τοῖς βεβήλοις ἀλλὰ τοῖς ἁγίοις[3].

James of Edessa in the 7th century, writing to Thomas the Presbyter on the conduct of public worship, says:

"After this they have delivered that the priest ought to testify to the people and admonish them and say, 'These HOLY

[1] St Chrys in Matt. c. ii, Migne, P.G. lvii. c. 80, in Heb. c. x., Migne, lxiii. c. 133.
[2] St Cyril-Al. in Joan. c. xx., Migne, P.G. lxxiv. c. 696. Cf. also St Cyr Al. in Joan. c. vii., Migne, lxxiii. p. 700 καθαροὶ γὰρ μᾶλλον καθαρῶς μεθέξομεν τοῦ Χριστοῦ, κατὰ τὸ ἐν ταῖς ἐκκλησίαις εὐρύθμως ἀναφωνούμενον, 'τὰ ἅγια τοῖς ἁγίοις'
[3] Vita S. Euthym. Analecta Græc. 1. p. 63.

THINGS of the body and blood are given TO THE HOLY and pure, not to them that are not holy[1].'"

While saying this the priest elevates the mysteries and shows them as a testimony to the people. See also the words of Symeon of Thessalonica quoted on p. 49[2].

Thus the interpretation placed upon these words from the 4th century onwards, and by writers of various churches, is that they served a purpose similar to that of the invitations and warnings contained in the Exhortations of the Anglican service, or, to use a still more modern illustration, of the "fencing the tables" practised in the Presbyterian Church of Scotland.

Turning to the internal evidence of the Liturgies themselves, we cannot expect to find in them such direct and explicit interpretation. They are the *lex orandi* not the *lex credendi*, and interpretation is incidental and indirect. What we should naturally expect would be that the context in which the words τὰ ἅγια κ.τ.λ. are found should be thoroughly consistent with this interpretation. We now proceed to examine the evidence on this point.

(1) In the immediate context we find *prayers for the holiness of the communicants*. The need of emphatic insistence on this was peculiarly important

[1] Brightman, p. 492.

[2] A very early anticipation of the words may be traced in the third Eucharistic prayer of the *Didache* εἴ τις ἅγιός ἐστιν, ἐρχέσθω· εἴ τις οὐκ ἐστί, μετανοείτω. Μαρὰν ἀθά. ἀμήν. c. 10

when all present (if we except one class of penitents, the *Consistentes*) were obliged to communicate. Thus the phrases ἁγίασον ἡμᾶς, εἰς τὸ ἁγίασαι ἡμᾶς, ἅγιοι ἔσεσθε ὅτι ἐγὼ ἅγιός εἰμι[1], occur just before or after the deacon has cried Πρόσχωμεν, and before the words τὰ ἅγια κ.τ.λ. It is *the double consecration of the gifts, and of the recipients of the gifts*, that forms the predominant note of this part of the service.

(2) When these words have been pronounced by the priest they generally meet with a response from the people, which is *a solemn confession of faith on their part in answer to this appeal*. The usual form is

εἷς ἅγιος, εἷς Κύριος Ἰησοῦς Χριστὸς εἰς δόξαν Θεοῦ Πατρός[2],

but sometimes it is a fuller expression of faith in the Trinity,

εἷς πατὴρ ἅγιος, εἷς υἱὸς ἅγιος, ἐν πνεῦμα ἅγιον[3].

Very similar to this is the use of the Nicene Creed in the Mozarabic Missal (see p. 97 f.), where it is avowedly placed after the elevation and before the Lord's Prayer, in order to prepare the hearts of the people by this act of faith for the worthy receiving of the Body and Blood of Christ. It is true that the words "Sancta sanctis" do not appear at precisely the

[1] Liturgies of Syrian St James, St Mark, St Basil, and St Chrys.

[2] Liturgies of the *Apost. Constit.*, Syrian St James, Syrian Jacobites, St Basil, St Chrys. &c.

[3] Liturgies of St Mark, Coptic Jacobites, Ethiopic Church, Abyssinian Jacobites, &c.

same point in the service, for in the Mozarabic Rite they have been turned to a different use, as explained in the foot-note[1]. What is pertinent to our enquiry is the unique fact that, in response to the elevation after the Canon (which is "*so as to be seen by the people*"), the congregation recite the Nicene Creed followed by the Lord's Prayer. This use of the Creed is peculiar to the Mozarabic service, but illustrates the Eastern response named above.

The foregoing evidence from early writers, and from the Liturgies themselves, tends unmistakably to the conclusion, that the words τὰ ἅγια κ.τ.λ. constituted an invitation to communion, and a warning lest any should receive it while unprepared.

[1] Migne, lxxxv. pp. 117 f. The words "Sancta sanctis" occur in the Mozarabic Missal, but in a different context and with a different meaning. After the Lord's Prayer comes the ceremony of *Commixtio*, at which the priest lets the particle of the bread fall into the chalice, saying, "Sancta sanctis. Et conjunctio corporis domini nostri sit sumentibus et potantibus nobis ad veniam &c." It is true that the position of the "Sancta sanctis" is shortly before communion, but the words, as they now stand, evidently refer to the commingling of the two species, which also appears from the fact that the form "Sancta *cum* sanctis" occurs in some French missals. Martene, I. IV. Art 9, § 2, T i. p. 412.

Yet it may be conjectured that originally it had the same meaning in the Gallican as in the Eastern rite. It may not have held the same marked position as an introduction to communion which it held in the East, and when the communion of the people became more rare, its significance was obscured, and a new reference connecting it with the Commixture arose. Its place may also have been slightly changed.

It is however held by some writers that the Eastern elevation was not primarily directed to this purpose, but had a God-ward, or sacrificial, intention. Such a theory necessarily involves a different interpretation of the formula which we are discussing, and it is suggested that τοῖς ἁγίοις, if masculine, may be descriptive of the Persons of the Trinity, before whom the gifts are elevated, or, if neuter, of "the holy places" or heavenly sanctuary, with reference to Heb. ix. 12, and to the symbolical presentation of a sacrifice before the throne of God.

Archdeacon Freeman in his *Principles of Divine Service* supports this view of the Eastern elevation and of the accompanying words. His theory of the elevation is thus given : "The Elements, one or both, were *lifted up* towards heaven with mysterious words, desiring they might be received up to God's heavenly and spiritual altar[1]."

This naturally involves a different meaning of the "mysterious words" (τὰ ἅγια κ.τ.λ.) from that which has hitherto been considered. Accordingly Archdeacon Freeman places an entirely different interpretation upon them. The passage is as follows:

"This is prefaced mostly by a prayer that God would receive this 'hymn,' and followed by the short Creed just described. It cannot, therefore, primarily have meant 'holy things are for holy persons,' which indeed would require ἅγια ἁγίοις. It

[1] Freeman, *Prin. of Div. Ser.*, Part ii. 175 f.

EASTERN LITURGIES

was rather a renewal, with reference to *reception*, of the lifting up which had before been made, either at oblation or consecration; an acknowledgment of the awful relations of nearness in which the Gifts, being what they were, stood either to the Three Persons of the Holy Trinity, or to the Holiest Place. This would act as a warning to the unfit, and as such it had come to be used. Such would seem, at least, to be the nature of the singular action and words in question, though there is some uncertainty about it[1]."

The strongest ground on which this interpretation rests is that the words are "prefaced mostly by a prayer that God would receive this 'hymn.'" But only two Liturgies (St James and St Mark[2]) are named as containing it, and both the use and the immediate reference of the word "hymn" are too indefinite to justify the statement that τὰ ἅγια κ.τ.λ. "cannot therefore primarily have meant 'holy things are for holy persons,'" especially as in the Liturgy of the *Apostolic Constitutions* the words are introduced by the express direction that the Bishop is to address them to the people: καὶ ὁ ἐπίσκοπος προσφωνησάτω τῷ λαῷ οὕτως, τὰ ἅγια τοῖς ἁγίοις.

Again, the elevation at τὰ ἅγια κ.τ.λ. is on this theory brought into relation with "the lifting up which

[1] *Ib.* Part ii. c. 2, p. 375.
[2] The passage from the Liturgy of St Mark is as follows: πρόσδεξαι τὸν ἀκήρατον ὕμνον ..παρ' ἐμοῦ βοῶντος καὶ λέγοντος, [ὁ λαός] Κύριε ἐλέησον, (3 times) [ὁ ἱερεὺς ἐκφώνως] τὰ ἅγια τοῖς ἁγίοις, [ὁ λαός] Εἷς Πατὴρ ἅγιος, εἷς Υἱὸς ἅγιος, ἓν Πνεῦμα ἅγιον εἰς ἑνότητα Πνεύματος ἁγίου.

had before been made, either at oblation or consecration," of which it is regarded as a "renewal." But if our evidence be reliable, there is little or no testimony to any previous *elevation* at those times, although the sacrificial idea was present.

Again, with regard to the grammatical meaning of the words, it cannot justly be said that "holy things are for holy persons" *would require* ἄγια ἁγίοις in Greek. The definite article in Greek has more varied shades of meaning than it has in English, and there is no valid objection to translating τὰ ἅγια κ.τ.λ. by " Such holy things are for holy persons."

Moreover, the passage quoted betrays the consciousness that the position of the words and ceremony is not that at which a sacrificial intention would be expected. The elevation is spoken of as "a renewal with regard to reception" of a previous lifting up at oblation or consecration, which are the times at which such a presentation to God would naturally occur.

It is to be regretted that Archdeacon Freeman, while stating with great clearness the view of the Greek elevation which he adopts, should have passed over these crucial words without a full discussion, while at the same time placing a very difficult meaning upon them. The meaning unreservedly assigned to the words by such writers as St Cyril and St Chrysostom is regarded by him as an afterthought, consequent upon the solemn and mysterious character of what he takes to be their primary significance. According to Archdeacon Freeman, the God-ward offering, thus expressed by word and action, would in itself become "a warning to the unfit," and so the later, but erroneous, interpretation would arise. Yet no other interpretation than that given by St Cyril and St Chrysostom appears to have been known in the 4th century, nor do any of the early writers on the Liturgies suggest the meaning which this writer defends

But it is fair to point out that there are several phrases in the Liturgies themselves, and in the immediate context of these words, which, if they stood alone, might lend support to some such interpretation.

In the Syrian Liturgy of St James the prayer following the elevation and preceding τὰ ἅγια κ.τ.λ. has these words, "Ἅγιε ὁ ἐν ἁγίοις ἀναπαυόμενος[1], and the same occurs in the Liturgy of St Mark. This might possibly be rendered, "Holy One, who abidest in holy places," but it is followed in both cases by the words "Ἅγιοι ἔσεσθε ὅτι ἐγὼ ἅγιός εἰμι, and the use of the word ἀναπαύεσθαι in other places suggests the meaning, "Holy One, who abidest in holy men."

Again, in the Liturgies of St Basil and St Chrysostom the words are preceded by a prayer to our Lord, Πρόσχες...ἐξ ἁγίου κατοικητηρίου σου καὶ ἐλθὲ εἰς τὸ ἁγιάσαι ἡμᾶς[2], where again, however, the predominant idea is that of the sanctification of the people.

[1] Brightman, pp 61, 138. [2] *Ib* p 341.

Once more, the reference of τοῖς ἁγίοις to the Persons of the Trinity may be thought to correspond to one of the responses made to the call τὰ ἅγια κτλ.— εἷς πατὴρ ἅγιος, εἷς υἱὸς ἅγιος, ἓν πνεῦμα ἅγιον. But if that most solemn of all interpretations of τοῖς ἁγίοις had been the original meaning of the words, it is not likely that there would have been the frequent variation of that response—εἷς ἅγιος, εἷς Κύριος Ἰησοῦς Χριστός. This reference to the Persons of the Trinity receives no support from early writers, nor does τοῖς ἁγίοις appear elsewhere to have been used in so sacred a relation.

If such considerations as these were corroborated by contemporaneous evidence, some weight might well be attached to them as indicating a possible meaning of the words, but *possible* interpretations, drawn from phrases in the Liturgies, while lacking external support, cannot stand in the face of the unhesitating testimony of writers from the 4th century onwards, supported, as it is, by equally strong evidence from the Liturgies themselves.

The Byzantine Liturgy of the Præsanctified (9th cent) contains the modified phrase,—τὰ προηγιασμένα ἅγια τοῖς ἁγίοις It is not easy to reconcile this phrase, occurring in this particular service, with Mr Freeman's interpretation of the words. This so-called "Liturgy," or "Mass," was a special form of administering the reserved Sacrament during the season of Lent, and especially on Good Friday, when the complete Eucharistic service seemed to many to be out of harmony with the penitential character of the season. The service is simply a form for communicating the people, and is characterised by frequent prayers for their sanctification It is a service of spiritual preparation leading up to communion, not one of sacrifice or memorial. Yet the elevation takes place, and is accompanied by the modified formula (τὰ προηγιασμένα ἅγια) and by communion.

Now the Liturgy of the Præsanctified was attacked (in A.D. 1050) by Cardinal Humbert on the ground that the gifts were thus doubly offered, once at the consecration, and again before communion. But this is not the case, for the service is not one of oblation, but of communion, and the whole tenour of the service is a significant guide to the true meaning of these words[1].

A difficulty however arises when we examine the translation of the words τὰ ἅγια τοῖς ἁγίοις into other languages of the East. The translations given by Mr Brightman in his *Liturgies Eastern and Western* are as follows. In the Syriac Liturgy of the Jacobite Church—"The holies to the holies." In the Ethiopic Liturgy of the Abyssinian Church—"Holiness to the holies." In the Persian Liturgy of the Nestorian Church—"The holy thing to the holies in perfection."

[1] Neale, *Hist. East. Church*, Introd. pp. 714, 725. Brightman, p. 351. It is a misnomer to speak of this service as a "Liturgy" or "Mass": it is merely an office for communicating the people with the reserved sacrament during a certain season.

In the Armenian Liturgy—"Unto the holiness of the holies." But Canon Venables and Archdeacon Freeman state the meaning of the Armenian version to be "The holy of holies[1]."

The difficulty of translation has evidently caused an ambiguity even greater than that which exists in the Greek form of the words, and it is not easy to decide what is the exact significance of these renderings into the Semitic, Persian, and Armenian tongues.

It does not seem possible to construct any theory from the translations, which we have given, that can weigh against the marked consensus of opinion as to the meaning of the words as interpreted by the Greek Fathers.

It is important that although the formula has been modified in Armenian, yet in the *Explicatio* of Khosroes (ed. Vetter, Friburg, 1880, p. 51) the following explanation is given, "Hoc est sanctitas, sed sanctis et mundatis solis qui confessione et lacrimis se ipsos a peccatis purificaverunt, hoc est ad sanctitatem."

There seems therefore to be no sufficient reason for swerving from the interpretation of the words τὰ ἅγια κ.τ.λ. which was placed upon them from the days of St Cyril and St Chrysostom. External evidence is wholly in its favour, and the balance of internal evidence from the language of the Liturgies inclines in the same direction. If this be the true

[1] Brightman, pp. 101, 237, 296, 447. *Dict. Chr. Ant* s.v. Elevation. Freeman, ii. p. 375 n.

meaning of the formula, it leaves little doubt as to the meaning of the ceremony which so significantly illustrates it.

We now turn to the direct testimony as to the Eastern meaning of elevation, both from early writers, and from the Liturgies which have been preserved.

It has been noted above that the two words ἀναδεικνύναι (or ἀποδεικνύναι) and ὑποδεικνύναι are employed in connexion with the central part of the service of Communion. We saw that ἀναδεικνύναι, with its cognate substantive ἀνάδειξις, has a definite reference to the actual consecration of the elements, but that no ceremonial act beyond taking the bread into the hands seems to have been thought necessary.

On the other hand, ὑποδεικνύναι has reference to the later part of the service when the consecration is complete, and to the acts preliminary to communion. It would seem that as ἀναδεικνύναι has relation to a presentation to God, so ὑποδεικνύναι signifies presentation to man.

Its earliest use is in Pseudo-Dionysius whose writings are assigned to the 5th or 6th century.

Ἱερουργεῖ τὰ θειότατα, καὶ ὑπ' ὄψιν ἄγει τὰ ὑμνημένα διὰ τῶν ἱερῶς προκειμένων συμβόλων, καὶ τὰς δωρεὰς τῶν θεουργιῶν ὑποδείξας, εἰς κοινωνίαν αὐτῶν ἱερὰν αὐτός τε ἔρχεται, καὶ τοὺς ἄλλους προτρέπεται [1].

[1] Dion. Areop. *Eccles. Hier.* c. iii. § 2, Migne, *P.G.* iii. c. 425. Cf. pp. 440, 444.

The consecrated gifts (τὰ ὑμνημένα, quæ consecravit, Bona) are here described as being brought into view of the people After this ceremonial, described by the word ὑποδείξας, the communion follows.

Mr Brightman points out that the words καὶ...ὑποδείξας are omitted after συμβόλων in a parallel passage in c. 3, § 12, and that as the "unveiling" there follows, it is possible that the words may only refer to the unveiling. Whatever may be its exact reference, it is clear that the word ὑποδείξας denotes an unveiling or ostension of the gifts to the people after consecration, whether it implies an actual elevation or not[1].

In the 6th century Cyril of Scythopolis, in a passage where he describes how Euthymius (ob. 473), whose

[1] Brightman, p. 490 n. Bona (*Rer Lit.* L. ii c 13, 2) quotes the passage as evidence of elevation, confusing the purpose as most western writers do. Sala in his notes on Bona defends the reference to elevation at length against Basnagius who denied it. Basnagius laid emphasis on the Scholiast's words "*Forsitan* intelligit elevationem," and even Sala allows the passage "dubitanter interpretari." Basnagius thinks it refers "non de elevatione, sed de Eucharistiæ revelatione quæ fiebat, cum Sacerdos detegeret Sacramenta, quæ velo tecta erant." Sala points to the fact that ὑπ' ὄψιν ἄγει occurs twice (really three times), and refers this double reference to the two acts of unveiling and elevation—"utriusque cæremoniæ ab eo factam esse mentionem." Goar regards the position of ὑποδείξας immediately before communion as conclusive that the word signified some kind of displaying to the people. Goar, p. 145. The Scholiast on Dionysius (A.D. 645) hesitates as to the meaning of the passage, but plainly affirms the practice in his day,—" This is clear that the Chief Priest, lifting up the holy Bread, showed the Blessing, or Sacrament, saying *Holy*, &c." Scudamore, *Not. Euch.*, p. 683.

life he wrote, often saw angels ministering to him at the Eucharist, certainly uses ὑποδεικνύναι of an act which displayed the sacrament to the people, and which was accompanied both by lifting up of the hands and by the cry τὰ ἅγια τοῖς ἁγίοις

Ταύτης (ἀναφορᾶς) ἀπαρτισθείσης, τὰς χεῖρας εἰς ὕψος ἐκτείνας φέρων καὶ ὑποδεικνύων τοῖς πᾶσι τὸ οἰκονομηθὲν πρὸς τὴν ὑμετέραν σωτηρίαν μυστήριον μετὰ φωνῆς ὑψηλῆς εἰς ὑπακούειν παντὸς τοῦ λαοῦ, λέγει τὰ ἅγια κ τ.λ.[1]

The words bearing on elevation are somewhat obscure, but the Latin version given in the Benedictine edition seems fairly to represent their meaning,— "Manibus in altum extensis ferens et cunctis ostendens dispensatum ad nostram salutem sacramentum."

We have therefore in Cyril-Scyth. a witness of the 6th century to what Euthymius did when celebrating the Eucharist (in Syria) during the 5th century in

[1] I have quoted the passage as given in the Benedictine edition of Cyril-Scyth (*Analecta Græca*, i. p. 62). But it is quoted in Brightman, p 486, Scudamore, *Not. Euchar.* p. 683, and the *Dict. Chr. Ant.* i. p 605, from Coteleruis (*Mon. Eccl. Græc.* ii. p. 268, § 81) in a somewhat different form—ἧς καὶ συντελεσθείσης (ἀναφορᾶς) τὰς χεῖρας ἐκεῖνος πάλιν εἰς οὐρανὸν ἀνατείνων καὶ ὥσπερ αὐτοῖς ὑποδεικνὺς τὸ οἰκονομηθὲν τῆς σωτηρίας χάριν τῆς ἡμετέρας μυστήριον κ.τ λ. The Benedictine editor says that these are the modified words of Symeon Metaphrastes ("his interpolator," Scudamore), not the original words of Cyril *Anal. Græc.* Præf p. 2. It should be observed that the words ὥσπερ αὐτοῖς ὑποδεικνὺς take the place of the categorical ὑποδεικνύων, thus throwing a shade of uncertainty over the statement which does not exist in the original. Canon Venables (*Dict. Ch. Ant.* s v. Elevation) makes use of the modified phrase as making the reference to ostension to the people doubtful.

which he lived. He uses ὑποδεικνύναι of a showing the sacrament to the people, which is accompanied by elevation and the words τὰ ἅγια κ.τ.λ.

Anastasius Sinaita, Patriarch of Antioch (c. 600 A.D.), uses ὑποδεικνύναι in the same way of elevation for ostension to all who are present.

Μετὰ τὸ ἁγιασθῆναι τὴν θυσίαν ἐκείνην τὴν ἀναίμακτον ἀνυψοῖ τὸν ἄρτον τῆς ζωῆς καὶ πᾶσιν αὐτὸν ὑποδεικνύει[1].

In the letter of James of Edessa (see p. 34), the elevation before communion is spoken of as "a testimony" to all the people ("tanquam testimonium"). The ceremony is certainly regarded as having precisely the same reference as the words, and as evoking the usual response. His words are:

"After this" (the Lord's Prayer has shortly preceded) "they have delivered that the priest ought to testify to the people and admonish them and say, 'These holy things of the body and blood are given to the holy and pure, not to them that are not holy,' and while he testifies this and cries aloud, he raises the mysteries on high and shows them to all the people as if for a testimony, and the people immediately cry aloud and say, 'The one Father is holy' and the rest. And so they communicate in the mysteries[2]."

Once again, St John of Damascus (ob. c. 755) at about the same date speaks expressly of the elevation (ὕψωσις), and connects it with the people's response to

[1] De Sacra Synaxi, Migne, P.G. lxxxix c. 841 A.
[2] The letter is quoted by Brightman, p. 490 f., from Assemani, Biblioth. Orient. i. pp. 479—486.

τὰ ἅγια κ.τ.λ. Though the actual formula is not named yet the response is given as if to the elevation, which is thus identified in purpose with the words so closely associated with it. He says:

Ἐν τῇ ὑψώσει δὲ τοῦ ἄρτου τῆς εὐχαριστίας οὐ λέγομεν Τρὶς ἅγιος ἢ Τρὶς Κύριος, ἀλλ' Εἷς ἅγιος, εἷς Κύριος Ἰησοῦς Χριστός κ.τ.λ.[1]

Dionysius Bar Salibi (12th cent.) connects the elevation with the "carrying about" of the elements to the people, and with the words *Sancta Sanctis*.

"Sacerdos elevat et circumfert Sacramenta, clamans et dicens, Sancta Sanctis[2]."

Very distinct testimony is given by Symeon of Thessalonica (15th cent.) to the ceremony of elevation, as connected with the formula τοῖς ἁγίοις κ.τ.λ. and the invitation to communicate.

Ἐνδυσάμενος τοίνυν καὶ ἀνυψώσας τὸν ἄρτον, καὶ τὰ ἅγια τοῖς ἁγίοις ἀνειπὼν, ἐκεῖνος μὲν πρὸς τὴν θείαν ἐκείνην τῆς ἱερᾶς τραπέζης ζῶσαν τροφὴν ἁγίους ἅπαντας καλεῖ, 'τὰ ἅγια,' λέγων, 'τοῖς ἁγίοις[3].'

The evidence of Germanus is interesting from the symbolical meaning assigned to the ceremony—ἡ δὲ ὕψωσις τοῦ τιμίου σώματος εἰκονίζει τὴν ἐπὶ τοῦ σταυροῦ ὕψωσιν κ.τ.λ.[4] But the identity and date of

[1] *De Trisag.* 27, Migne, *P.G.* xcv. 57 [496]. Cf. *de Corp. et Sang.*, Migne, xcv. 409 [659], quoted p. 150.
[2] Renaudot, i. p. 267.   [3] *De Templo*, Goar, p. 228.
[4] Germanus, *Theoria Rer. Divin.* Migne, *P.G.* xcviii. p. 448 B. For account of probable author, see Migne, p. 15 f.

the writer are very uncertain. Bingham accepted the passage as from the patriarch of Constantinople, A.D. 715, but Canon Venables (*Dict. Chr. Ant.* s.v. Elevation) assigns it to "his namesake and successor five centuries later," A D. 1222. The elevation is connected by this writer with various crosses made in the air with both Bread and Cup so as to hallow all parts of earth and air. This in itself is unlike any early references. See the connexion of crossing with the Western elevation at "omnis honor et gloria," p. 84 f.

The evidence of the Liturgies themselves must now be examined. There is no trace of elevation in the *Apostolic Constitutions*, nor in the Egyptian Liturgies of St Mark or of the Coptic and Abyssinian Jacobites, nor in the Nestorian Liturgy (Persian). It is not found in the modern text (1869) of the Liturgy of St Basil, although in that of St Chrysostom of the same date it is clearly marked—ὑψῶν τὸν ἅγιον ἄρτον ἐκφωνεῖ τὰ ἅγια κ.τ.λ. The 9th century Liturgy of St Chrysostom bears no trace of it.

No weight need be given to its omission from the Liturgy of the *Apostolic Constitutions*, since it does not represent a living rite, though it has a literary value as representing the form of the current Syrian Liturgy, probably at the close of the 4th century.

Nor can we argue from its absence from other early Liturgies that no such ceremony was in use, as the rubrical directions lack much detail. But the omission may fairly lead us to the conclusion that it was not regarded as essential, or as having strong and universal tradition to support it. Such statements as that of J. S. Durantus, based on the evidence of the Greek Fathers, that the Church elevated the Eucharist from its very cradle, receive no real support from the witness of the Liturgies[1].

It is expressly named in the Syrian Liturgy of St James,—$ὑψῶν τὸ δῶρον$: in the Byzantine Liturgy of St Basil (9th century),—$ὑψοῖ τὸν ἅγιον ἄρτον$: and in the 9th century Byzantine Liturgy of the Præsanctified,—$τὸν ἄρτον ὑψῶν$[2].

This review of the evidence leads to the conclusion that in the 5th or 6th century there was a definite displaying of the consecrated gifts to the people before communion, and that from the 6th century at latest this displaying took the form of elevation. The Liturgies bear this out so far as their evidence goes, but silence need not always imply the absence of a ceremony, and those Liturgies which contain the elevation probably represent a tradition earlier than the 6th century.

Again, the connexion with the words $τὰ\ ἅγια\ κ.τ.λ.$ is very clearly marked, and we have seen reason to conclude that before the end of the 4th century they were generally understood to mean "Holy things are

[1] Bona, *Rer. Lit.* II. 13, § 2.
[2] Brightman, pp. 61, 341, 351.

for holy persons." If so, the elevation which accompanied them must have had a similar significance. The combined purpose of both words and act was to present "a testimony" to the people, and to prepare them for communion. In short, (1) the elevation was not Godward but for the people, and (2) its immediate purpose was to invite the worthy and warn the unworthy immediately before the time of communion, stirring to reverent devotion and fervent thanksgiving.

Two objections, however, remain to be considered which traverse both these ideas of the Greek elevation. One denies that the elevation was made in view of the congregation. The other allows this popular use, but materially alters the spiritual purpose.

(1) An important objection has been made that the Greek elevation cannot have been before the people, since the elevation "took place within the Bema, the doors of which being closed and the curtains drawn, it could be only seen by the attendant ministers[1]." This is also the opinion of Goar who says, "non ita tamen ut a populo conspiciatur Dominicum Corpus elevat Græcus sacerdos[2]." Renaudot's words—"Orientalium disciplina est elevare et *astantibus* ostendere sacra mysteria"—have been taken to

[1] *Dict. Chr. Ant.* s.v. Elevation.
[2] Goar, *Eucholog.* p. 145, n. 158. Cf. pp. 84, 151.

support the same view, on the supposition that he limited "astantibus" to those within the Bema[1].

It is true that the structure of a Greek Church, with its Bema or Sanctuary separated and screened off by doors and curtains, hid *the actual consecration* from the gaze of the congregation. But it is also true that we have evidence of a formal withdrawal of the curtains so that the communion of the people might follow. It is therefore quite possible, and, in the presence of other evidence, probable, that the elevation took place after that withdrawal.

The consecration out of sight of the people is expressly named in the *Anaphora* of an Egyptian Liturgy (found in the Arabic *Didascalia*, c. xxxviii.). The Bishop is to consecrate, "the veil being let down, and the presbyters and the deacons and the subdeacons being within[2]." But this need only refer to what was treated as the more solemn part of the service, and was held as a mystery hidden from all without the Bema.

---

[1] Renaudot, ii. p. 608. Scudamore (*Not. Euch.* p. 683) says, "I presume that the *astantes* are only those about the altar." But Latin writers use "astantibus" in a wider sense. Thus Bonaventura describes the Roman elevation "et fidelibus adstantibus ostendit" (ed. Mogunt. vii. p. 78): in the Carmelite Missal, "in tantum ut omnibus adstantibus convenienter appareat" (*Tracts on Mass*, p 244). Cf. "circumstantibus" in the *Indutus Planeta* (*ib.* p. 186). Also in the *Directorium* of Ciconiolanus, "Hoc pro doctrina adstantium sic proferebam" (*ib* p. 210).

[2] Brightman, p. 511.

The withdrawal of the veil is expressly named by St Chrysostom as taking place after the sacrifice and while the consecrated gifts are being brought forth for the communion of the people. This is the time of the appeal τὰ ἅγια κ.τ λ. and of the elevation. He says:

'Ενταῦθα ἐκφερομένης τῆς θυσίας, καὶ τοῦ Χριστοῦ τεθυμένου, καὶ τοῦ προβάτου τοῦ Δεσποτικοῦ, ὅταν ἀκούσῃς Δεηθῶμεν πάντες κοινῇ, ὅταν ἴδῃς ἀνελκόμενα τὰ ἀμφίθυρα, τότε νόμισον διαστέλλεσθαι τὸν οὐρανὸν ἄνωθεν, καὶ κατιέναι τοὺς ἀγγέλους[1].

St Chrysostom does not say expressly *when* the veil was withdrawn, but he marks it as a time to be looked for with the most intense expectation and devotion. We are at least warranted in claiming that the view we have adopted of the elevation, which certainly was current a century or two later, gives the natural explanation of St Chrysostom's words, and that the veil was withdrawn at the latest when the consecration was complete[2].

I have not noticed the words δεηθῶμεν πάντες κοινῇ in any Liturgy: probably St Chrysostom is not quoting exactly, but in rhetorical language describes

[1] *In Ephes.* Hom. iii. 5, Migne, *P.G.* lxii. p. 20. Cf. also *in* 1 *Cor.* Hom. xxxvi. 5, Migne, lxi. 313.

[2] Duchesne alludes to the veil, which, he says, "shut out the view up to the moment when after the dismissal of the catechumens and other non-communicants, the celebration of the mysteries in the presence of the initiated only was begun." This apparently means that the veil was withdrawn at the commencement of the *Missa Fidelium*, i.e. before the *Anaphora* was commenced. This theory would still more completely dispose of the objection. *Chr. Worship*, p. 85.

the climax of the service when the people first see the gifts prepared for such holy service. In all Eastern Liturgies the deacon summons the people to earnest and reverent attention before the τὰ ἅγια κ.τ.λ. is uttered, and the elevation made[1], and there is no part of the service which so closely corresponds to the idealised picture given by the great orator as that which follows the consecration. It is surely a *petitio principii* to say, without express evidence to that effect, that because the veil was drawn to hide the consecration, it hid the elevation also. The suggestion has a late Western ring, for while in the West it would be impossible to hide the consecration without hiding the elevation also, in the East a considerable interval intervenes, during which the veil was probably withdrawn, and communion with its preliminary preparation made possible.

(2) One other consideration remains. The Greek elevation is referred to by various liturgical writers of the Roman Church, and is claimed in support of the later Western elevation which was made the signal for the adoration of the Host.

Such writers allow that the Eastern *time* of elevation was not that of the Western Church, but, its acknowledged *purpose* being to exhibit the now consecrated elements to the people, they do not regard the exact point of time as material. Elevation imme-

[1] πρόσχωμεν, or μετὰ φόβου θεοῦ πρόσχωμεν

diately after consecration is, however, regarded as more suitable, on the ground that no delay should take place in rendering devout homage to Christ as present upon the altar.

It is true that the purpose of the Eastern elevation is to show the Sacrament to the people, and it is reasonable to claim that the difference of time, so long as the consecration is complete, does not affect the question of adoration: but no single passage, of those which we have examined in the Greek authors, suggests any idea of worship directed to the consecrated gifts.

It was not until the 17th century that the Greek Church accepted formally the doctrine of Transubstantiation, and the consequent adoration of the elements. In the *Confessio Orthodoxa* (1643), which is a formal exposition of the teaching of the orthodox Greek Church, after an express acceptance of the doctrine of Transubstantiation, it is stated that "therefore we ought to honour and adore the Holy Eucharist as our Saviour Jesus Himself." Also in the *Confession of Doritheus* (1672) it is even more strongly stated that "the Body and Blood of the Lord in the Sacrament of the Eucharist ought to be superlatively honoured and worshipped with *latria*. For the worship of the Holy Trinity and of the Body and Blood of the Lord is the same[1]." This insistence upon the highest kind of

[1] Kimmel, P. i. pp. 126, 460. See Scudamore, *Not. Euch.* p. 684 f.

worship (*latria*) is very significant of later Western influence. In the earlier history of the Eastern Church neither the doctrine nor its consequences find any place.

It is therefore impossible to attach any weight to the assertions, made by Durantus, Sala, and Bellarmine, that the *rationale* of the Greek elevation was identical with that of the Roman Church immediately after consecration. A discussion of the passages, on which they base their contention that St Ambrose, St Chrysostom, and St Augustine encouraged the adoration of the Host[1], lies beyond the scope of this enquiry; but with their contention that the Greek ceremony of elevation was identical in purpose with that of the Roman Church, we are more closely concerned. It is enough to say that they quote for this purpose the same passages from Basil, Dionysius, and Germanus which have been given above. Other Roman writers, such as Bona, Goar, Renaudot, question the use made of these passages, and rest their arguments upon the doctrinal statements of such writers as St Ambrose and St Augustine. These are regarded as claiming for the Eucharist the same adoration as that due to the true Body of Christ[2].

[1] See Bingham, *Christ. Ant.* xv. c. v. § 5 for a discussion of these passages.

[2] "At testimoniis Ambrosii l. 3 de Spiritu sancto, cap. 12, Augustini in Psalmum 98 [*adorate scabellum*], Theodoreti in Dialogo Ἀσυγχύτως, Cyrilli Catechesi Mystagogica v., et quibusdam aliis

Neither of the two objections, which have now been discussed, is of sufficient weight to induce us to alter those conclusions at which we have already arrived.

We have now seen how the words τὰ ἅγια τοῖς ἁγίοις significantly interpret that part of the service which immediately precedes communion, and of which the elevation is the leading ceremony. A Liturgy provides two things which are essential to the fulfilment of our Lord's institution—the commemoration and the communion. These are the two parts of the one great act which the due celebration of the Lord's Supper involves, and which in the Eastern rite, as in the Anglican, are never divided. The one provides for the sanctification of the elements, the other with equal insistence provides for the sanctification of those who are about to receive them.

The elevation, with its accompanying formula, links together these two parts. When the prayer of consecration is over, further prayers are offered for the sanctification of communicants, and the priest, lifting up the holy food[1], cries "Holy things are for holy persons."

There is nothing which exactly corresponds to this

probati contendimus, eos Eucharistiæ non minus quam veræ Christi carni τεθεωμένῃ adorationem deferendam censuisse." Renaudot, i. p. 269.

[1] The actual point of time is not invariable.

in the Roman Missal, although, as we shall see, the elevation in the Western and Mozarabic rites at the close of the Canon has probably a common origin and meaning with that of the Eastern Liturgies[1].

But in the *Ritus Celebrandi Missam* attached to the Pian Missal (1570) there is an elevation so similar to the Eastern ceremony that it will be convenient to consider it at this point of our enquiry. The directions there given for the communion of the people are as follows:

"Postea genuflectens accipit manu sinistra pyxidem seu patenam cum Sacramento, dextera vero sumit manu particulam, quam inter pollicem et indicem tenet aliquantulum elevatum super pyxidem seu patenam, et conversus ad communicandos in medio altaris dicit, *Ecce Agnus Dei, Ecce qui tollit peccata mundi.*"

This elevation is of late origin[2] as are also the words which accompany it, but it bears a close resemblance to the Eastern ceremony. Both are acts of ostension after consecration to the communicants, both are signals of the approaching communion, and in neither is any express direction given for the adoration of the elements[3].

[1] pp. 97—99.
[2] See Add. Note, p. 60.
[3] It is, however, practically impossible to detach this Elevation from the whole idea of the Roman Elevation of the Host. Although there is no express direction to adore, yet wherever definite devotion to the consecrated Elements is inculcated, this ceremony must inevitably suggest it.

The contrast however between the words used at or about the elevation is full of interest. In the East the relation between the holiness of the recipient and the sacred character of the food thus elevated is the predominant thought. In the West attention is centred upon the tremendous mystery believed to have taken place at consecration, and the signal for communion is given by the solemn and sacred words, "Ecce Agnus Dei, Ecce qui tollit peccata mundi."

So regarded, the Eastern elevation, severed on the one hand from the idea of sacrificial use, and on the other from any thought of adoration beyond that of our Lord Himself present in His own appointed means of grace, stands out in bold relief as a significant action, interpreting by outward symbol the inner meaning of the words which it accompanies.

ἅγια τὰ προκείμενα...
ἅγιοι καὶ ὑμεῖς...
τὰ ἅγια οὖν τοῖς ἁγίοις κατάλληλα.

Additional Note on the Roman Elevation and Formula used at Communion.

It has been thought best for the purpose of comparison to notice by anticipation this particular form of the Roman elevation with its unique form of words. I am not aware of any evidence earlier than the 16th century of either the ceremony or the words being thus employed. The Report of the Royal Commission on Ecclesiastical Discipline (1906) says of the use of the words *Ecce Agnus Dei, Ecce qui tollit peccata mundi,* "The practice has no sanction from antiquity: nor does there appear to be any evidence that it was ever customary in the English Church before the Reformation." This is true of the Western Church as a whole, and both words and ceremony are of late Roman origin. The use of these words as an invitation to intending communicants must be carefully distinguished from the *Agnus Dei* of the mediæval Missals, which is an anthem addressed to our Lord ("Agnus Dei qui toll*is*..." not "Ecce Agnus Dei...qui toll*it*"). In the Stowe Missal, where Mr Warren regards the words not as the technical *Agnus Dei*, but as one of several verses sung *during Communion*, it is singular that the form is *Ecce...qui tollis*. "Toll*is*" may be a scribal error for "toll*it*," but as it stands it looks like a confusion between the older form used immediately after the *Commixtio*, and the later used at the time of actual Communion. The conclusion arrived at by Mr Warren is interesting as illustrating the use made of the verse by Cranmer in 1549[1]. See below.

The nearest approach to such a use in the Anglican

---

[1] *Liturgy and Ritual of the Celtic Church*, p. 242. In his note on p. 266 Mr Warren regards the verse as the *Agnus Dei* of the old Missals. He has courteously allowed me to state his more recent conclusion.

Church was in the 1st Prayer Book (1549), where after the Canon, and before reception, the priest says:

> "Christ our Paschal lamb is offered up for us, once for al, when he bare our sinnes on hys body upon the crosse, *for he is the very Lamb of God that taketh away the sinnes of the world.*"

At the same date the anthem *Agnus Dei*, taken from the Sarum Missal, was appointed to be sung "in the Communion time...beginning so soon as the priest doth receive the holy Communion." The change from the Missal is significant, for there it was sung after the Canon and *Commixtio*, but *before* the communion of either Priest or people, while in 1549 it was appointed to be sung *during the time of Communion*[1].

It is singular to find that the Presbyterians at the Savoy Conference suggested the use of this formula at the consecration. See p. 176 f. It is also important to note that *apart from the presence of actual communicants* the ceremony and its accompanying words have no place even in the Roman service.

[1] This was carefully noted by Archbishop Benson in *Reid and Others* v. *Bishop of Lincoln*, pp. 54—60.

CHAPTER II.

WESTERN LITURGIES.

TURNING now to Western services we find the enquiry to be a much more complicated one. Elevation is found in the mediæval Missals of the Latin Church in five different positions, which we may, for the sake of convenience, again enumerate.

(1) At the Offertory.

(2) At the " Qui pridie " and " Simili modo."

(3) Immediately after the words of consecration.

(4) At the close of the Canon ("omnis honor et gloria ").

(5) At the communion of the people—a late elevation introduced in the 16th century. See p. 60.

Two of the above, (1) and (2), have already come under notice in the Eastern rite; both (4) and (5) have some resemblance to the Eastern elevation before communion; (3) is without a parallel in any other service.

(1) *Elevation at the Offertory.*

As in the East so in the West the offering of the people's gifts to God was a prominent feature in the Eucharistic service. It was a fulfilment of the Apostolic order, "To do good and to distribute forget not, for with such sacrifices God is well pleased." Accordingly "the Offertory," or anthem sung while the people were offering, has come to hold a very definite and important position, and the term is often used of the whole action of that part of the service.

In such a position the ceremony of elevation, as a formal act of presenting the gifts, is so simple and obvious, that we should expect to find it occurring very early and very generally. Yet it is not so in the Eastern Liturgies, although great attention was paid, not only to the preparation of the elements in the Chapel of the *Prothesis*[1], but also to the "Great Entrance," at which the elements were solemnly placed upon the Holy Table.

In the West, though elevation for this purpose is more clearly marked, yet it is of late introduction into the rubrics, and even then is not universal. The offerings were laid upon the Lord's Table and thus symbolically placed at His disposal, but, beyond that, very often no ceremony was added.

[1] For instances of elevation at the *Prothesis*, see p. 10.

It is, however, to be remembered that rubrics more generally follow custom than create it, and the appearance of the express direction to elevate the unconsecrated gifts is probably an indication that such a ceremony had for some time been gradually coming into use.

In the earlier Western services there is no trace of such a custom. We have careful accounts given of the services at Rome in the 8th and 9th centuries, both in the *Ordines Romani*, and also in the writings of Amalarius, a Gallican ritualist who visited Rome in A.D. 832 in order to pursue his liturgical studies.

Duchesne describes minutely the ceremonial as gathered from these sources. "The faithful, including not only the laity, but also the priests and other clerics, together with the Pope himself, brought each their gifts of bread and wine, for each was obliged to make his own offering. The Pope himself, assisted by the bishops and priests, received the loaves; the archdeacon and his colleagues the *amulæ* or phials of wine." Out of these the bread and wine (mingled with water) for the Communion are placed on the altar, but no elevation is named, and no prayer accompanies the ceremonies. This was at Rome in the 9th century[1].

At an earlier date we have an account of the Gallican services from St Germain of Paris (ob. A.D. 576), who bestowed great care on matters connected with public

[1] Duchesne, *Christ. Worship*, S.P.C.K. pp. 173 f. For the *Ordines Rom. ib.*, pp. 456 f.

worship. The bread and wine were prepared beforehand, as in the Oriental rite, and brought in procession to the altar. They were there covered with a veil, and an anthem, called in the Mozarabic rite *Sacrificium* or *Offertorium*, was sung. No mention is made of elevation[1].

The idea of *separating* the elements to holy use is probably the origin of the variable Collects called in the Gelasian Sacramentary *Secretæ*, and in the Gregorian either *Secretæ* or *Orationes super oblata*. Amalarius understood the name to mean that they were said *secreto*, but Maskell holds that it probably arose "a secretione donorum et oblationum[2]." No corresponding ceremony of elevation however appears in connexion with them.

Even at the close of the 11th century the *Micrologus*, though it names two elevations during the Canon, describes no such ceremony when it speaks of the first oblation at the Offertory[3].

The English service-books present considerable variety of use, and we can trace in successive editions the gradual adoption of a distinct elevation at the Offertory, that of the Cup only being expressly named.

[1] *Christian Worship*, pp 205 f.
[2] Amalarius, iii. 20. Maskell, *Anc. Lit.* p. 101. See Martene, I. c. IV. Art. 7, p 393, who follows Amalarius.
[3] *Microl* c. xxiii., Migne, *P.L.* ch. c. 977 f. The work of an unknown author (*de ecclesiasticis observationibus*), who lived in the days of Gregory VII. (ob. 1085). *Ib.* p 975.

In the 13th century Sarum Ordinary the prayer "Suscipe sancta Trinitas" is termed "*Oracio post offerendum : dum calix collocatur,*" but that is all[1]. In the next century the Ordinary of the same Church contains the words: "*Assumat patenam cum pane et teneat in manibus et dicat* Suscipe &c.": also of the Cup, "*Accipiat calicem et teneat in manibus et dicat* Offerimus &c.[2]" But in the later Sarum and Bangor Missals, as edited by Maskell, the elevation of the Cup is expressly named. After the *Offertorium* the priest receives both chalice and paten (*calicem cum patena et sacrificio*) from the deacon, and this rubric follows: "*Et inclinato parumper elevet calicem utraque manu, offerens sacrificium Domino, dicendo hanc orationem,* Suscipe &c." The words seem to imply an offering of both elements, though the elevation of the Cup only is named. This is possibly explained by the rubric in the Hereford Use "*Sumat patenam cum hostia et ponat super calicem, et tenens calicem in manibus suis, dicat devote :* Suscipe &c.," that is to say, the priest held the Cup with the Paten and Host upon it, while saying the words of oblation[3].

We can thus trace three stages of development, (1) placing the elements upon the altar, (2) holding them in the hands during the prayer of oblation, (3) actual elevation. Yet the York service always

[1] *Tracts on the Mass*, p. 220.
[2] *Ib.* pp. 4 f.
[3] Maskell, pp. 78—85.

preserved the simplest form, "*componat hostiam super corporales pannos.*"

The same varieties of use are seen in several foreign service-books, which exhibit features differing from the normal use of Rome, and representing customs peculiar to certain Churches or conventual bodies.

The *Directorium* of Ciconiolanus, published at Rome in 1539, exhibits the same intermediate stage as that found in the 14th century Sarum Ordinary, and also in that of the Pian Missal. This latter fact corresponds with the statement of Gavantus that the *Directorium* furnished the rubrics of the Breviary of Pius V.[1]

In one edition of the *Alphabetum Sacerdotum*, representing a Gallican use at the end of the Middle Ages, we find the fuller direction "*levet calicem* (al. *surgat calicem*)" before "Suscipe Sancta Trinitas." The same elevation (the Cup only being expressly named), which was noted in the Bangor and later Sarum Missals, is also found in another Gallican Use (1557), namely of the Church of Coutances. "*Accipiens calicem in manibus, erigendo eum sursum, dicat* Suscipe &c.[2]"

In the *Indutus Planeta*, a series of directions for celebrating the Mass, printed in France during the early part of the 16th century, and claiming to represent the usage of the Church of Rome, the elevation of *both Host and Cup* is directed under certain conditions. "*Si*

[1] *Tracts on the Mass*, p. 207. Cf. pp. xxix. f.
[2] *Ib.* p. 41.

missa simplex conventualis vel privata fuerit, sacerdos accipit patenam cum hostia duabus manibus ibi mediocriter elevatis et dicit, 'Suscipe Sancta Trinitas.'" Exactly the same "moderate" elevation is directed *verbatim* for the Chalice[1].

Burckard's *Ordo Missæ* (published at Rome, A.D. 1502) is a work of much interest from its undoubted influence on the *Ritus Celebrandi Missam* prefixed to the Missal of 1570. It had papal approval, and marks a definite attempt to replace the scanty rubrics of the earlier Missals by fuller and more authoritative directions. Addis and Arnold (*Catholic Dictionary*, s.v. Rubrics) say that "it was Burckard...who first set out at length both the words and the ceremonies of the Mass." This influence is seen in the instance before us. The Offertory-Elevation never obtained any notice in the Roman *Ordinary*, but the *Ritus Celebrandi Missam* in directing the elevation of both Host and Chalice follows the rubric of Burckard, which directs that they should be separately elevated as high as the breast (*usque ad pectus*) while the words of oblation are being recited[2]. In the Mozarabic Missal, although strongly expressed words of oblation are used[3], there is no direction to elevate either element.

The evidence points to the existence of the Offertory-Elevation from about the 14th century, not as a matter

[1] *Ib.* p. 185.   [2] *Ib.* xxv. f., 149 f.
[3] "*Offert* sacerdos *hostiam* cum calice."

of obligation, but of fairly wide acceptance, and especially in the Churches of England and France.

The reference to a "Missa conventualis," in the passage quoted from *Indutus Planeta*, suggests the enquiry whether the Offertory-Elevation may have become more marked in the usage of some of the monastic orders. It would be dangerous to generalise from a few instances, but we find it definitely named in two such *Ordinaries*.

(1) In a French Dominican Ordinary, dated as early as the 13th century, there is an express direction to elevate the Chalice—"*et tenens (calicem) cum duabus manibus aliquantulum elevatum dicat*, Suscipe sancta Trinitas,"—but for the Paten the simpler direction is given—"*sumens patenam ante pedem calicis collocat Hostiam*[1]."

(2) In an English Charterhouse Ordinary of the late 15th or early 16th century, we again find the elevation of the Chalice, but not of the Host—"*elevans illum (calicem) reverenter utraque manu pectore tenus dicit*, In spiritu humilitatis...*Depositaque hostia super corporalia nichil dicendo vel faciendo, cooperit calicem corporalibus*[2]."

It is remarkable that in the *Rationale* of A.D. 1543, which explains in some detail the ceremonies of the Mass, no mention is made of any elevation at the Offertory[3]. It is clearly regarded as of much less importance than

[1] *Tracts on the Mass*, p. 78. Cf. p. xxi.
[2] *Ib.* p. 101. Cf. p. xxiv. [3] Collier, *Hist.* v. p. 117.

the later elevation after consecration, which had then come to be part of the central action of the Mass.

It would therefore appear that at first the simple placing of the gifts upon the Holy Table was in itself regarded as a presentation of them before God. A later development was the holding them in the hands of the priest at the recital of a prayer of oblation, while the final stage was the moderate elevation, sometimes of the Cup only, sometimes of both Host and Cup, as an act of offering to God.

Nothing can be more simple or significant than this formal and ritual presentation of our gifts to God. In the early ages of the Church such offerings were in kind and of the most varied nature, though later canons allowed the presentation of those gifts alone which were for use in the Communion. The Church of England, at the last revision of the *Book of Common Prayer*, revived in a measure the older and wider offering, by a rubric which orders the placing of all the gifts upon the Holy Table, and which enjoins that our "alms and oblations" be offered with our prayers to God. It is, however, very doubtful whether the history of the word "oblations" allows us to include the elements in that term, which seems to denote the "*other devotions of the people*" as distinct from the "*alms for the poor*[1]."

[1] See Bishop Dowden's article in the *Journal of Theological Studies*, April, 1900. On the other hand it is contended that the rubric directing the bread and wine to be "placed upon the Table" was added in 1662, when the word "oblations" was also added.

We may here notice that the language used at the Offertory in several of the Eastern Liturgies, and in the Western Ordinary, suggests that in earlier times there was not the same sharp distinction between the offerings made before, and after, the consecration as has been made in later times. The Offertory prayers in the Syrian Liturgy of St James and in the Persian (Nestorian) rite speak of the elements as being then a sacrifice not merely Eucharistic, but in some sense for the blotting out of sins[1]. Duchesne speaks of the oblation in the Gallican Liturgy as having "bestowed on it by anticipation the same honour which it had after consecration[2]." In the Roman Missal the prayer at the first oblation runs thus:

"Suscipe, sancte Pater...hanc immaculatam hostiam quam ego...offero...pro innumerabilibus peccatis...meis, et pro omnibus circumstantibus, et pro omnibus fidelibus...vivis et defunctis, ut mihi et illis proficiat ad salutem..."

In the same way the words at the Offertory in the Mozarabic rite are "*Offert sacerdos Hostiam cum Calice*[3]."

It is at least worth consideration whether this significant use of words was really proleptic, or whether it arose from the fact that, in the age when these prayers took shape, the elements were, from the time they were placed upon the Holy Table, regarded as presenting to view the memorial of our Lord's sacrifice. See pp. 145 f.

[1] Brightman, p. 46 35 b, 47. 34 b, 48. 14 b, 273. 14.
[2] *Christian Worship*, p. 204.   [3] Migne, *P.L.* lxxxv. p. 112.

(2) *Elevation at "Qui pridie" and "Simili modo."*

This is the first of three clearly marked acts of elevation during the Canon of the Western service. Of these both the first at "Qui pridie" and "Simili modo," and the last at "Omnis honor et gloria," are of distinctly earlier date than the elevation immediately following the words of consecration. They both have this feature also in common, that neither of them is historically connected with the later adoration of the Host, being of earlier origin than the express enunciation of the doctrine of Transubstantiation, an event which distinctly modified the purpose of elevation.

One interesting difference between these two earlier forms will appear in the course of our enquiry. The elevation at "Qui pridie," which is thoroughly characteristic of the English Canon, disappears from other Western services before the Reformation: on the other hand the elevation at "Omnis honor et gloria" is not named in the English uses, although we shall find evidence which might suggest that it was a popular practice.

The elevation at "Qui pridie" and "Simili modo," that is, at the very opening of the words of institution and before consecration, arose naturally out of the words "took bread" as illustrating our Lord's own action. At first it is most probable that nothing was done beyond the simple "taking" necessary in order to adapt the

Priest's action to his words. But, as we have seen in the Eastern Liturgies, the original form of words received additions, some of which are also found in the Western Canon. For instance, the Western rite contains the words "in sanctas et venerabiles manus Tuas, et elevatis oculis in cœlum, ad Te Deum Patrem suum omnipotentem, Tibi gratias agens," although it has nothing which corresponds to the following words so suggestive of a sacrificial purpose—"stretched them forth to heaven," "showing it unto Thee, the God and Father"—which we have traced in several Eastern Liturgies (p. 19).

And yet, while the Eastern forms direct no corresponding action on the part of the celebrant (except in later copies), the Latin rite, *while omitting the words, directs the action*. In the East, we have found no clear direction to elevate until the Canon is ended, but in the West, the opening words of the recital of the Institution have been accompanied, from at latest the 11th century, by an express order to elevate slightly both the Bread and the Wine.

No evidence of this elevation occurs in the *Ordines Romani*, or in the records of early Gallican use. But the following passage from the *Micrologus* clearly shows that, at the close of the 11th century in Western Europe, elevation was practised at "Qui pridie" and "Simili modo," and was closely connected with the blessing of both elements.

"Deinde panis in manus accipitur, et antequam reponatur in altare benedicitur; item et calix elevatus ante depositionem benedicitur. Nam et Dominus in Evangelio utrumque legitur benedixisse antequam dimitteret e manibus. Accepta enim in manibus benedixit, postea discipulis dedit[1]."

It might at first sight appear that the use of "elevatus" in the case of the Cup meant no more than the necessary lifting in order to take it into the hands (cf. "in manus accipitur" of the Bread). But in ch. x., which treats of the veiling and unveiling of the Cup, it is expressly directed that the Cup be *elevated unveiled*, both here and at "per ipsum et cum ipso," this reason being given—"et hoc fortasse ideo, quia cautius levatur sine operimento quam coopertus." See p 114.

The simple "taking the Cup" for blessing, as recorded in the Gospel, is thus ritually developed into more definite elevation, and with express reference to our Lord's words and action

In ch. xxiii., where directions for celebration are given, the elevation of both elements at "per ipsum et cum ipso" is described, but this earlier ceremony at "Qui pridie" and "Simili modo" is not named. It would therefore seem that the later elevation at "per ipsum" &c. was definitely ordered by this time, while that at "Qui pridie" and "Simili modo" was not of obligation.

[1] *Micrologus*, c. xv "*De acceptione oblationis in manus.*"

At the beginning of the 12th century two writers of the Gallican Church (Honorius and Hildebert) refer to the elevation at "Qui pridie" &c., though the reference is not so clear as in the *Micrologus*.

Honorius, Bishop of Autun, describing the several parts of the Western Canon, says in a passage following the account of "Quam oblationem" and the words of Institution,

"Exemplo Domini accipit sacerdos oblatam et calicem in manus et elevat, ut sit Deo acceptum, sicut sacrificium Abel...et sicut sacrificium Abrahæ...et sicut Melchisedek...[1]"

An account is next given of the section "Unde et memores," which immediately follows the recital of the Institution.

The context indicates an elevation closely connected with the words of consecration, while the express words "Exemplo Domini[2]," and "accipit...et elevat" point to the "Qui pridie" and "Simili modo" elevations, rather than to the later Roman form. This is confirmed by the absence of any ostension to the people, and the definite purpose "ut sit Deo acceptum," which in some Eastern rites is apparent at the manual acts.

The other passage is in a Latin poem by Hildebert, Bishop of Tours, and afterwards of Le Mans (Cœno-

[1] Migne, *P.L.* clxxii. p. 793 D.
[2] The "example of our Lord" naturally refers to the words "took bread" in the Gospels.

mansis), where he describes in detail the service of the Mass.

"Panis in hoc verbo, sed adhuc communis, ab ara
    Sumitur, et sumptum tollit utraque manu.
Nec prius in mensam demittit quam tua, Christe,
    Verba repraesentans explicet ista super.
        * * * * * * *
Hic levat et calicem, signatque, nec ante reponit
    Quam super auctoris verba retractet ita."

The meaning of elevation is subsequently given:

"Presbyter idcirco, cum verba venitur ad illa,
    In quibus altari gratia tanta datur,
Tollit utrumque notans quod fit communibus escis
    Altior, et quiddam majus uterque gerat[1]."

The exact reference has been disputed, but it seems beyond doubt that it is to the "Qui pridie" elevation, and not to the later Roman form. The Bread is taken up from the altar at the opening words of the Institution, and elevated, not *after* the words "Hoc enim est corpus," but *during the whole recital.* The same extended elevation is carefully named at the consecration of the Cup.

At the same time the presentation to God is not expressly named, but the ceremony seems intended to represent to the people the fact that at the words of consecration ("cum verba venitur ad illa, In quibus &c.") the common bread and wine become a more excellent food.

[1] *Carmen de Offic. Miss.*, Migne, *P.L.* clxxi. pp. 1186 f.

The insistence on the elevation being continued to the end of the recital, and its more public significance, may foreshadow the coming change when the earlier lifting up, "ut Deo sit acceptum," gives place in the Roman rite to the elevation "ut videatur a populo[1]."

Direct testimony to this practice is also found in a Constitution of Odo, Bishop of Paris (A.D. 1197), where it is contrasted with the elevation at the words "Hoc est corpus," and *a moderate elevation only allowed*, lest the two ceremonies should be confused.

"*Præcipitur presbyteris ut cum in Canone Missæ incœperint* 'Qui pridie quam pateretur' *tenentes hostiam ne elevent eam statim nimis alte, ita quod possit ab omnibus videri, sed quasi ante pectus detineant, donec dixerint,* 'Hoc est &c.' *et tunc elevent eam ut possit ab omnibus videri*[2]."

In the Council of Würzburg (A.D. 1298) the same careful distinction is made, and the earlier act at "Qui pridie" is not regarded as an "elevation"—

"*Non elevent eam (Hostiam), sed ante pectus detineant donec dixerint* 'Hoc est &c.' *et tunc elevet eam decenter, ita ut possit videri*[3]."

That such cautions were not unnecessary appears from a very unusual form found in a 13th century Missal of the Ursinensian Monastery, where a rubric at "Qui pridie" directs, not the ordinary moderate

---

[1] Cf. the 13th century Ursinensian Missal quoted below, where extreme elevation takes place at "Qui pridie," and no elevation occurs after consecration. This also seems to indicate a transitional stage.

[2] Mansi, xxii. p. 682.   [3] *Ib.* xxiv. p. 1187 E.

lifting up, but extreme elevation of the Bread. The words are "*quantum potes eleva dicens*, 'Accepit panem[1],'" so that the Bread must have been made visible to the people *before consecration*. When we remember that the words of the service could not be intelligently followed by the mass of worshippers, it is not surprising that the fear arose lest such extreme elevation might be taken as a signal for that worship which, according to the new teaching, should *follow*, but on no account *precede*, the consecration.

In the same century Durandus, in giving reasons for elevation after consecration, repeats the same caution[2]: and later on at the Council of Frisingen (A.D. 1440) it again appears[3]. In consequence of this the earlier elevation at "Qui pridie" and "Simili modo" came to be omitted in most of the Western Missals, except those of the English Church: and Mr Maskell says, "nor has it been admitted into the Roman use [lest] ill taught people among the laity might naturally fall into the error of untimely adoration[4]."

[1] No elevation is directed in this Missal after consecration. Gerbert, 1. p. 361.

[2] "Ut populus, *non præveniens consecrationem*, sed ex hoc cognoscens illam factam esse, et Christum super altare venisse, reverenter ad terram prosternantur." *Rationale*, iv c. 41, § 51—53.

[3] "Nec hostiam ante consecrationem in altum quomodo elevare (præsumat), ne adorando hostiam non consecratam populum idololatriam committere contingat." Gerbert, 1. p 362.

[4] Maskell, *Lit. Ch. Eng.* p. 134.

In most of the English Uses this earlier elevation at "Qui pridie" and "Simili modo" is expressly ordered, but is carefully limited in extent—"aliquantulum," "modicum" (Sar. 13th cent.), "parum ab altari" (Sar. 14th cent.), "paululum" (later Sarum, York, and Bangor). In the Hereford Use no elevation is named beyond the primitive "Sumat sursum," and in a Charterhouse Missal (15th or 16th cent.) "accipit utraque manu" is the only direction given[1].

Mr Maskell also notes that some editions of the Sarum Manual, which contain the Canon, have the following rubric which expresses the same minute caution as that found in continental writers

"Et elevet hostiam parumper ita quod non videatur a populo ...quia si ante consecrationem elevetur et populo ostendatur, sacerdotes sicut fatui faciunt populum idolatrare adorando panem purum tanquam Corpus Christi, et in hoc peccat[2]."

On the Continent, elevation at "Qui pridie" and "Simili modo" appears in a (French) Dominican Missal of the 13th century, with the same limitation as to extent—"aliquantulum," "modicum" : in the Carthusian statutes (as given in Martene[3]),—"parum": in the *Alphabetum Sacerdotum* (France, 15th or 16th cent.),—"ante pectus": and again in the *Indutus Planeta* (of the same date and country),—"parum."

---

[1] Maskell, pp. 132—142. *Tracts on the Mass*, p. 101.
[2] Maskell, p. 133.
[3] Martene, I. c. iv. Art. xii. Ord. 21, p. 597.

In the Coutances Missal (A.D. 1557) there is no mention of any elevation at this point. But it is of greater significance to find it absent from Burckard's Missal (1502), as its influence on the Missal of Pius V. is undoubted, and in that Missal (1570) it does not appear[1]

Thus where a Church or Order used its freedom to have local variations in minor details, the moderate elevation at "Qui pridie" &c. often remained. But in a book which seems to have borne more of the stamp of authority, such as Burckard's Missal, it gives place to the greater elevation which immediately followed the consecration.

We are therefore justified in concluding that the elevation at "Qui pridie" and "Simili modo" can certainly be traced in Western Europe from the close of the eleventh century, and most probably existed as a widespread custom at an earlier date. We can connect its origin, without hesitation, with the desire to do as our Lord Himself did at the original Institution when He "took bread," and "in like manner after supper took the cup." At first, the elevation was probably only that necessary for the manual acts of receiving the elements into the hands for consecration, as the following phrases testify:—*accipit duabus manibus—accipit in manibus dicendo—accipit utraque manu* —no further elevation being enjoined.

[1] *Tracts on the Mass*, pp. 44, 62, 80, 156 f., 186. The Missal of 1570 is that of the Church of Rome at present.

But just as the original words of the Evangelists received additions, which were believed to represent authentic tradition, and served to produce a more vivid picture of the original scene, so the ceremonial action which represented the original manual acts of our Lord Himself became enlarged, and the simple ceremony of "taking bread" and "taking the cup" developed into a formal and definite elevation.

At this point of the service, therefore, the ceremonial must be studied in close connexion with what our Lord Himself did at the original Institution, so that in this respect the elevation at "Qui pridie" and "Simili modo" differs from all other forms of that ceremony. Yet one singular development has been that whereas the manual act of "fraction," which is of undoubted authority, entirely disappeared from the ceremonies at consecration many centuries before the Reformation, that of elevation, which is of late introduction and often of uncertain significance, was at one point or another retained.

The matter is one of interest in relation to the Anglican Office, where exactly the converse has taken place. Elevation is nowhere named[1], and was expressly forbidden in the Prayer Book of 1549. But the primitive form of fraction was restored in 1662.

We have already noticed the careful distinction

[1] I.e. beyond the direction "Here the Priest is to take the Paten into his hands."

made between the lesser elevation before consecration and the greater elevation when it is complete. This distinction deserves special notice as being significant of the marked change which came over Eucharistic ceremonial in the 12th and 13th centuries, and was due to the doctrine of Transubstantiation which had been formally decreed in A.D. 1215.

When that doctrine was sanctioned by authority the adoration of the consecrated elements naturally followed, and took the place of that devout and reverent use of them which had hitherto sufficed. Extreme elevation was now ordered immediately after consecration, with a view to adoration, while genuflexion or prostration was its natural complement on the part of both priest and people.

Moreover the change of substance was now so definitely located as the immediate result of the words of consecration, that it became necessary to guard against any mark of adoration before those words were completed.

This caution marks the rise of a very material and local view of Christ's presence in the Sacrament. It expresses a much more narrow idea than that of Cardinal Newman's words, in which he explains the manner of that presence:

"But if place is excluded from the idea of the Sacramental Presence, therefore division or distance from heaven is excluded also, for distance implies a measurable interval, and such there cannot be except between places Moreover if the idea of distance is excluded, therefore is the idea of motion Our Lord then neither descends from heaven upon our altars, nor moves when carried in procession. The visible species change their position, but He does not move[1]"

For those who impose upon Christ's presence in the Eucharist the limitations of distance, time, and place, such caution as to the *time* of elevation is but reasonable, but these limitations find no support in the earlier forms of service, where our Lord is rather thought of as present throughout the rite, ministering to and receiving the devotion of His people.

(3) *Elevation at "Omnis honor et gloria."*

We have now to consider the Western elevation at the close of the Canon. It is very similar in position to the Eastern elevation, but takes place *before* the Lord's Prayer, not *after* it as in all Liturgies of the Eastern Church. It will be more convenient to discuss its history and meaning before we come to the great Roman elevation *immediately* after consecration, because it is distinctly the earlier ceremony of the two.

This elevation at "Omnis honor et gloria" is closely connected with "the crossings" which accompanied the closing words of the Canon. These were most elaborate, and consisted of the crossing of the Chalice with the Host eight times at certain carefully specified words.

[1] *Via Media*, ii. p. 220 (ed 1877).

These "crossings" are found in all the Western Missals after the words "Per quem hæc omnia, Domine, semper bona creas," and appear in the Sarum Canon of the 13th and 14th centuries, even though no elevation is there ordered. The same is true of the other English Missals, and the express mention of this elevation is one of the distinguishing marks of foreign services as distinct from English.

This fact that "the crossings" are universal and found in copies where no mention of elevation occurs, suggests the thought that the *elevation* came in subsequently to "the crossings." At the same time it must be remembered that in the *Ordo Romanus I*.[1] (c. A.D. 800) an elevation at "Omnis honor" is named without express mention of the usual signing with the cross. The use of the cross, however, in connexion with the celebration of the Sacraments dates from the end of the 4th century[2], while in the ritual books of the Latin Church from the 8th century onwards precise rules are laid down as to the number of crosses to be made at several points of the service[3]. The frequent use of the sign of the cross may therefore have preceded the elevation at this point, as it certainly did in other

---

[1] Duchesne, *Christian Worship*, p. 461. Cf. p. 464, where the crossing may be indicated by the words, "levat duas oblatas *et tangit ex ipsis calicem*."

[2] St Aug. *Tract.* cxix. *in Johan. Evan.* c. xix. St Chrys. *Hom.* liv. *in St Matt.* c. xiv.

[3] E g. from the *Ordines Romani* onward.

parts of the service, and if we were able to fix definitely the meaning of "the crosses" it would throw light on the meaning of this particular elevation.

Just as in "taking the bread" at the "Qui pridie" a certain lifting up was necessary, so in crossing the Chalice with the Host one, if not both, of the elements had to be lifted from the altar, and an elevation, incidentally necessary to the action, took place. Thus in the Hereford Use this rubric follows "the crosses"— *Tunc reponat corpus*, the Chalice having also been raised in the priest's hand, but I have noticed no mention of any specific elevation in this or in any other of the English Uses. It is therefore possible that the elevation at "Omnis honor" was evolved from what was probably the earlier ceremony at this point, namely "the crossings."

One marked feature of this Western ceremony is that both Host and Chalice were elevated *together*[1], the Host being generally lifted up above the Chalice. This is said to be represented on certain coins which are described on pp. 154 f., and it also is expressly directed in many rubrics at this point of the service.

Roman writers on ritual acknowledge that this was an earlier form of elevation than that which immediately followed the words of consecration. Bona, a strong upholder of the later Roman elevation, allows that it

[1] This would also naturally follow, as both elements were taken up for the ceremony of crossing

finds no support in the old Sacramentaries, or in the *Ordines Romani*, and that Alcuin, Amalarius, Walfridus Strabo, and the *Micrologus* do not name it. On the other hand he notes that the *Ordines Romani* do mention the elevation at the close of the Canon, as do Amalarius, the *Micrologus*, and others[1].

Again Sala, in his notes on Bona, challenges the assertion made by Thiers that St Chrysostom makes a reference to the elevation after consecration, thinks that in this Thiers "hallucinatum fuisse," and mentions others who thought "that it was introduced later than the custom of elevating the host at the words 'omnis honor &c.'"

In short it is an acknowledged fact that the older post-consecration elevation was at the close of the Canon, and (speaking generally) at the words "Omnis honor et gloria." There was, however, a considerable variety of usage as to its exact position, it being sometimes connected with the Lord's Prayer which shortly followed.

This was therefore the chief elevation in the Roman rite, until the elevation after consecration was introduced. From that time it came to have less importance and was called "the lesser elevation" (*elevatio minor*)[2], and in France "la petite élévation"

[1] "Ea dumtaxat in *Ordine Romano* elevatio commemoratur qua calix attollitur ante Orationem Dominicam." Bona, *Rer. Lit.* II. 13, § 2.

[2] Gerbert, I. Disq. IV. XXXVI. p 372.

The earliest mention of it is in one of the *Ordines Romani* in the 8th century. The passage is given by Duchesne—"Et dum venerit pontifex ad *omnis honor et gloria* levat duas oblatas in manus suas, et diaconus calicem tenens et levans paululum usque dum dicit: *Per omnia sæcula sæculorum, Amen*[1]."

Closely connected with the evidence of the *Ordines Romani* is that of Amalarius who wrote *De Officiis Ecclesiasticis* in A.D. 830, and frequently cites the *Ordo Romanus I.*[2] He describes a service at which the archdeacon elevates the Cup (i.e. to the priest), having first carefully veiled it, thus obtaining a foremost rank among the deacons, as Joseph did among the disciples through his care for our Lord's burial. In the same way the priest who elevates the Bread (*oblata*) represents Nicodemus who prepared our Lord's body for the sepulchre. After explaining the crosses made by the Bread on the Cup, he adds "Christi depositionem de cruce monstrat elevatio sacerdotis et diaconi[3]."

Le Brun des Marrettes (de Moleon) confirms this witness of the ancient Roman *Ordo*, which, he says, agrees with the ancient "Ordinary" of Rouen. He remarks that neither contains any mention of the separate

[1] Duchesne, *op. cit.* p. 461. See also p. 464. Bona (*Rer. Lit.* L. ii. c. 13, 2) in describing this says, "cum dixerit (archidiaconus) 'per ipsum et cum ipso' levat *cum offertorio calicem* per ansas, &c." "Offertorium" stands here for "oblatæ," just as the word "Offertory" is now commonly used of the offerings of the people.

[2] Duchesne, p. 147.

[3] Ap. Hittorp. p. 199. Amalar. L. iii. c. 26. Cf. Gerbert, i. p. 372.

elevations of the Host and Chalice (séparément), but only of that which was made immediately before or at the *Pater noster*[1].

There is therefore no room for doubt as to *when* the elevation in the old Roman *Ordines* took place, or as to its being that of both species in one ceremonial act.

Rabanus Maurus (9th century) says, "Elevatio sacerdotis et diaconi corporis et sanguinis Christi elevationem ejus ad crucem insinuat." Two things locate this reference to the later elevation at the close of the Canon:—the reference to the combined action of priest and deacon (cf. *Ordo Romanus*) and the fact that it was of both Body and Blood[2].

In the 11th century the *Micrologus* describes the Mass of Western Europe, and gives an account which in this matter corresponds to that in the *Ordo Romanus*. It describes no elevation immediately after consecration, but later on after "Omnis honor et gloria" it gives this rubric, "*Hic elevat oblatam cum calice dicens,* 'per omnia sæcula sæculorum...' *Et deponit oblatam cum calice dicens,* 'Oremus. Præceptis salutaribus moniti...audemus dicere, Pater Noster*[3].*'"

[1] "Il n'est fait aucune mention de l'Élévation de l'Hostie et du Calice séparément : mais seulement de celle qui se fait immédiatement avant le *Pater* ou au *Pater*." De Moleon, *Voyages Liturgiques*, p. 287.

[2] Rab. Maurus, *de Cler. Instit.* i. 33 (*Add. de Miss*), Migne, cvii. p. 324.

[3] *Micrologus*, c. 23. Cf. c. 10, "Discooperitur tandem (calix) dum levatur ubi dicitur *Accepit et hunc..* et ibi, *per ipsum et cum ipso*."

In the same century (1070) we have this witness of John, Bishop of Avranches: " Oratione finita uterque calicem levent et simul deponant et cooperiant[1]." The "oratio" is probably the Canon; "uterque" corresponds to the combined action of priest and deacon as in the *Ordo Romanus*; the covering of the chalice agrees with what is described in the *Micrologus*[2]. The annotator in Migne's *Patrologia* adds that formerly not only the chalice was elevated, but also "hostia in patena calici super posita." It is further noted that the writer (John, Bishop of Avranches) says nothing of elevating the Body "seorsim," as was done in the annotator's day after consecration and for adoration.

Early in the 12th century Ivo, Bishop of Chartres, in describing the crosses made at the elevation by the priest and deacon, distinguishes them from those made at an earlier part of the service. The former, he says, had relation to the change made in the elements, or to their salutary purpose: the latter, being accompanied by the elevation of both Host and Chalice, commemorated the crucifixion according to our Lord's words " cum exaltatus fuero a terra, omnia traham ad me ipsum," while the replacing of both elements upon the altar signified the honourable burial by Joseph and Nicodemus[3].

The Bread is not named in c. 10 as the writer is speaking specially of the covering or uncovering of the chalice.

[1] Migne, *P.L.* cxlvii. pp. 36, 78   [2] See p. 89, n. 3.
[3] *Epist.* 231, Migne, *P.L.* clxii. p. 234.

At the close of the same century (1184) Hugo de S. Victore, Bishop of Paris, continues this line of testimony, and once more identifies this particular ceremony of elevation as connected with that of the crosses. The idea of an open displaying of the glory of God as shown in the passion of Christ is also clearly marked. He says:

"Et ut ostendat sacerdos qualiter per Christum gloria Trinitati sit acquisita in mentibus fidelium, post signa crucis utraque manu elevat sacramentum Corporis et Sanguinis Christi, et paulo post deponit, quod significat elevationem corporis Jesu Christi in cruce et ejusdem in sepulchrum depositionem[1]."

(For the evidence of the *Expositio Missœ* ascribed to Bonaventura see p. 152 f.)

The evidence so far adduced shows that, as compared with the elevation at "Qui pridie," the elevation at "Omnis honor et gloria," i e. at the close of the Canon, can claim earlier testimony and more continuous support. No earlier notice of the former appears than that of the *Micrologus* of the 11th century, while the latter is named in the *Ordo Romanus*, three centuries before. Moreover, when the actual course of the celebration is described in the *Micrologus* (c. 23), only the elevation at "Omnis honor et gloria" is named. It seems fair to conclude that, prior to the custom of elevation immediately after consecration (i.e. to the 12th or 13th century), this elevation at the close of

[1] Migne, *P.L* clxxvii. p. 435 A.

the Canon was the most prominent elevation of the Roman Mass.

We proceed to notice the very varied position which this particular elevation occupied. De Moleon speaks of it as taking place in the Church of Rouen *at or before the Lord's Prayer*[1]. As a matter of fact, while its most frequent place was at "Omnis honor et gloria," or at "per ipsum et cum ipso et in ipso," we also find evidence of its being continued from these words into the Lord's Prayer; or again, of its being commenced after "Fiat voluntas tua," the elements being raised at "sicut in cœlo" and replaced at "et in terra." The last named use is from a Missal of the Church of Lyons, and looks like the fanciful variation of some irresponsible ritualist, who adapted the raising and replacing of the elements to the celestial and terrestrial fulfilment of God's will[2].

A more simple use and one of obvious significance was that of elevating at "panem nostrum." This was seen at Vienne when Martene and Ursin Durand visited that church about A.D. 1710, and it is also named by de Vert as seen at Lyons. This use has at least a plea of reason, for it probably arose out of a special application of the words "daily bread," and also of our Lord's declaration in St John vi. 51: "The bread

[1] De Moleon, *Voyages Lit.* p. 95. See above, p. 88 f.
[2] *Ib.* p. 58, "Conformément au sens de ces mots."

that I will give is my flesh which I will give for the life of the world[1]."

There are instances also of this elevation being placed as late as the *Embolismus* (or expansion of the last clause of the Lord's Prayer), after the words "libera nos a malo." Coming thus at the end of the Lord's Prayer, the showing of the consecrated gifts seems to have signified what it did at a somewhat similar place in the Eastern service, namely, a warning that " holy things are for holy persons." It is so placed in the *Alphabetum Sacerdotum*, a French work of the 15th or 16th century. After the people have given the usual response at the close of the Lord's Prayer,—" Libera nos a malo," the priest elevates the paten and says, " Amen." Then follows the *Embolismus*,—" Libera nos quæsumus Domine ab omnibus malis, &c." In the Coutances Missal (1557) an elevation is found at the same words, as well as at "Omnis honor et gloria[2]."

We come now to some passages which bear more directly upon *the purpose* of this elevation. Burckard's *Ordo Missæ* (c. 1500) directs that it is to be followed by genuflexion and veneration of the Sacrament on the part of the priest[3], and the same direction is given

[1] See *Tracts on the Mass*, pp. 241 f., where a number of these later variations are given.

[2] *Tracts on the Mass*, pp. 47, 65. The varied position of this elevation tells against any essential connexion with a particular form of words. But originally it seems to have been connected with " the crossings."

[3] " Usque ad terram genuflectens sacramentum veneratur." *Tracts on the Mass*, p. 159.

in the *Ritus Celebrandi Missam* of the Pian Missal. In the Coutances Missal of 1557, the words "omnis honor et gloria" are followed by the rubric *Hic ostendat populo hostiam*; and a Missal of the Church at Sens gives a similar direction,—*Ostendat populo hostiam de manu dextera*. The same public exposition at this point is found at Nevers,—*Elevans Calicem cum Hostia et ostendens populo dicit*, Omnis honor: and at Lyons,— *ut a populo adoretur:* and at Cordova,—"*ut a circumstantibus cerni adorarique possit.*" Moreover in the Premonstratensian Missal, published at Paris in 1578 (fol. 146), the elevation is continued from "Omnis honor et gloria" to the beginning of the Lord's Prayer, *ut adoretur Christus oblatus in hoc augustissimo Sacramento pro omnibus*[1].

Thus this elevation seems to have been almost universal in the Roman Church, though never expressly enjoined in England. There is, however, a Missal in the Fitzwilliam Museum, Cambridge, written in France during the 14th century, and prepared for the use of some Pope, in which no elevation after "the crosses" is enjoined[2].

It is singular that so marked and widespread a ceremony should find no express notice in the English

---

[1] *Ib.* pp. 84, 241, where a number of instances are given of "la petite élévation" in French and Spanish churches.

[2] Fitzwilliam Mus., McClean, 51. It was probably written for one of the Popes at Avignon.

service-books[1]. But it is evident that the action of the priest in making the "crosses" was such as to be visible to the people, and that the ceremony was used for the avowed purpose of gazing at the Sacrament. In mediæval times the ordinary use of the Mass gradually ceased to be for communion, and the popular idea of attending Mass was to witness the elevation and adore the Sacrament. The communion of the people was an accident of the service, not part of the central event in it Further, it is evident that the ceremony of frequently crossing the Chalice with the Host (whether with or without elevation) was regarded as a "second sacring."

This is illustrated by Becon's words in his "Displaying of the Popish Mass":—"What shall I say of daunsing your little great God aboute the Chalice with *per Ip, et cum Ip, et in Ip, SUM*, which followeth the praying for the dead? That is so holy a thing that it is called the second sacring, and may by no means be left undone[2]."

The popular view appears still more clearly in "A dialogue or familiar talk betwene two neighbours" (Rouen, 1554). "The bel tolleth, I have lost sacring, a vengeaunce on it, with babling with the. But yet I trust to see my maker daunce about the cuppe."

[1] This probably marks a measure of independence of Rome retained by some local Churches, and especially by the Church of England. Cf. p. 132.

Works, Parker Soc. III p. 277.

And again in "The Resurrection of the Mass" printed at Strasbourg in the same year,

> "But heare ye? When the second sacrynge comes
> And your yonge God is dandled about the chalice,
> Looke that then ye start up with good devotion
> And to honour your God most humbly deuyce[1]."

The painful manner in which so sacred a subject is thus handled, however superstitious and mistaken the view which the writers condemn, does not alter the value of the evidence to the fact that the crossing of the Chalice was held, at least in the popular mind, to be for the purpose of displaying to the popular gaze some aspect of the great mystery of the Mass.

The singular and isolated case of the Mozarabic Liturgy, as restored at Toledo by Cardinal Ximenes in the early years of the 16th century, has already been referred to in connexion with the Eastern elevation (see p. 36 f.) There is no doubt that it represents the ancient use of the Church in Spain which had been suppressed by Gregory VII. in the 11th century in order to establish the Roman use. It has a close affinity with the ancient Gallican service, and, like it, bears unmistakeable marks of correspondence with the Eastern Liturgies[2].

[1] Quoted in *Tracts on the Mass*, p. 264.
[2] The development of ritual between the 2nd and 4th centuries, which led to this correspondence between the Liturgies of the East and of Gaul, does not concern our enquiry See Duchesne, pp. 32 f, 88 f., 90 f

The Mozarabic rubrics enjoin elevation, both after consecration, and between the Canon and the Lord's Prayer. The former does not now concern us and is dealt with on pp. 133 f The position of the latter bears a close resemblance to that of the Western elevation at "Omnis honor et gloria," as well as to the Eastern elevation after the Lord's Prayer.

The Canon of the Mozarabic Missal does not end, as in the normal Western form, with the ascription of praise, "est Tibi Deo Patri...omnis honor et gloria," at which the elevation usually takes place, but with a prayer for the blessing of the elements. At its close the priest summons the people to a confession of faith, elevates the Host in full view of the people, and the Nicene Creed, followed by the Lord's Prayer, is then recited, so as to form a short office of immediate preparation for communion This position of the Nicene Creed is unique. The passage is as follows:

"*Dicat presbyter:* Fidem quam corde credimus ore autem dicamus. *Et elevet Sacerdos corpus Christi, ut videatur a populo Et dicat Chorus symbolum,* Credimus in unum Deum "

The purpose of the elevation is here clearly marked as similar to that of the Eastern elevation, namely, to be seen by the people, the positions of both being very similar The object of those who introduced the Nicene Creed is also beyond doubt, as we learn from the 2nd Canon of the 3rd Council of Toledo in A.D. 589[1].

[1] Mansi, lx. p. 993. The adoption of the Nicene Symbol, with the newly added "filioque," took place at this Council, and was

"Priusquam Dominica dicatur oratio, voce clara a populo decantetur [Symbolum Constant.], quo fides vera manifestum testimonium habeat et ad Christi corpus et sanguinem prælibandum pectora populorum fide purificata accedant."

This confession of faith, following closely upon the act of elevation in sight of the people, has an exact counterpart in the confession made in the Eastern Liturgies to the call of the celebrant τὰ ἅγια τοῖς ἁγίοις (see pp. 36 f.). We are justified in concluding that the Mozarabic elevation which follows the Canon bears closer analogy to the Eastern elevation than to that of any Western rite which we have to consider, notwithstanding the strangely different use of the words *Sancta sanctis* which we have already pointed out (p. 37).

The relation of these two elevations may be thus stated: *They differ* (1) in the exact position of the ceremony, the Eastern elevation *following*, and the Mozarabic *preceding*, the Lord's Prayer, (2) in the position and meaning of the words *Sancta sanctis*. *They agree* (1) in the general position at the close of the Canon, (2) in the purpose of ostension to the people, yet with no idea of adoration directed to the elements, (3) in the response, or Creed, which follows the elevation, the purpose of which was to prepare the people for a worthy communion.

mainly due to the renunciation of Arianism by the Visigoths, though political reasons are also thought to have had considerable weight in the adoption of the words "filioque."

Thus the points of agreement outweigh the points of divergence, and we have no hesitation in advancing the opinion, especially in view of the distinctly Oriental characteristics of the Gallican services, that the Mozarabic elevation has a similar origin and purpose to that of the Eastern Liturgies.

But further, it is difficult to resist the conclusion that the Western elevation at the words "Omnis honor et gloria" belongs to the same line of ritual development. All three are post-consecration ceremonies; all three occur at the close of the Canon; all three, so far as external evidence leads us, are for the purpose of showing the elements, now consecrated, to the people before communion[1]; and (except in the case of some later Missals) there is no suggestion of that form of adoration which marked the rise of the doctrine of Transubstantiation.

It is, however, to be noted that the joint elevation of Host and Chalice, and the elaborate "consignationes" accompanying it, which are so characteristic of the elevation at "Omnis honor et gloria," are not found in either the Eastern or Mozarabic rite.

The evidence on the whole leads to the conclusion that the joint elevation of both elements at the close of the Canon can claim the support of earlier testimony than any other form of elevation in the Western

[1] This will be discussed in relation to the Western elevation at "Omnis honor," &c. on pp. 151 f.

Church. We can trace it back to a date not later than the 8th century, where it appears in the *Ordines Romani*, and this early witness is confirmed by that of Amalarius and Rabanus Maurus in the following century. Its resemblance to the Eastern elevation and to that of the Mozarabic rite is an important fact which must not be forgotten when we come to consider the inner meaning of the ceremony.

(4) *Elevation at, or immediately after, the words of consecration.*

This elevation is as distinctly characteristic of the Western Church as that which accompanies the *Sancta sanctis* is of the Eastern. Its origin is of much later date, and its history can be traced with greater clearness than that of any other form of Western elevation, which is partly due to the well-defined doctrinal purpose which fostered and controlled its development.

The elevation of the Host, or, to state the matter more fully, the elevation of the consecrated elements separately (*seorsim*) after the consecration of each, was unknown for at least a thousand years after Christ. This is freely allowed even by Roman authors, who claim, however, that the main purpose of elevation after consecration is always the same (namely to evoke adoration), and that the change made between the

11th and 13th century was not one of essential character, but merely of *position*.

We have found earlier evidence of the elevations at the Offertory and at "Qui pridie," and of the post-consecration elevation at "Omnis honor et gloria," but the act of separate elevation of the Bread and Wine *immediately after consecration* finds no notice until the 12th century. Thus the *Ordines Romani* and Amalarius know nothing of it in the 8th and 9th centuries. The *Micrologus* in the 11th century does not allude to it, nor does an Ursinensian Missal of the 13th century quoted by Gerbert[1]. In the rubrics of the York Missal the elevation of the Host *never* obtained a place, though a slight elevation of the Cup is directed. (This, however, may be an accidental omission. See p 108 n.)

This practice is said by Mabillon to have arisen in Gaul in the second half of the 11th century ("post medium sæculum XI videtur fieri cœpta[2]"). I have been unable to trace any actual mention of it until the late 12th century, but as the specific direction of a canon or rubric usually follows after a fairly wide adoption of the custom, we are justified in placing the actual rise of the practice at a somewhat earlier date. Its birthplace was clearly in Gaul, and as the Gallican

[1] Gerbert, i p. 361.
[2] Mabillon, *Comment. Præv. in Ord. Rom.*, Migne, *P.L.* lxxviii. p. 877.

Church of the 11th century was specially affected by the teaching of Berengarius against Transubstantiation, it is thought probable that the ceremony, which certainly came to be regarded as a public protest against his views, took its rise about that time. From the end of the 12th century it took firm root in Gaul, and then spread to other countries, until it was at last adopted by the Church of Rome as the authorised ceremony which was intended to call forth the most marked expressions, not only of reverent respect, but of clearly defined worship.

In examining the evidence of the rise and purpose of this form of elevation, it will be necessary to deal with that of the Host and Chalice separately, the actions being quite distinct, and the elevation of the Host having a much more marked character. The lifting up of the consecrated wafer above the head of the celebrant was the especial opportunity given for what came to be popularly spoken of as "seeing their Maker."

The history of the elevation of the Chalice is also more complicated than that of the Host, owing to the rise in some Churches of a still later form of its elevation at the words "Hæc quotiescunque feceritis, in mei memoriam facietis."

In the canons of synods and orders of Bishops the ceremony is for the most part connected only with the elevation of the Host, but probably the elevation of the Chalice is included, though not actually named. We shall, however, see later on that the latter ceremony was not universal.

(1) *Elevation of the Host.*

The earliest mention of such elevation is probably that found in the statutes of the Carthusian Order, which were drawn up about the middle of the 12th century. After naming the earlier elevation at "Qui pridie" &c., the following rubric occurs:

"Dicto autem 'Hoc est Corpus meum,' elevatur hostia, ita ut possit videri, et pulsatur campana uno ictu aut pluribus in missis tantum conventualibus[1]."

At the word "benedixit" the Chalice is also elevated, but only a little (*parum*), and so held until the end of the clause "Hæc quotiescunque[2]." Prostration at the elevation of both Host and Chalice is ordered.

In A.D. 1197 a more general order is found in the Constitutions of Odo of Paris (quoted on p. 78), where a moderate elevation only (*ante pectus*) is directed at "Qui pridie," but after "Hoc est enim Corpus" a more extreme elevation "*so that it may be seen by all.*"

Again in A.D. 1204 and in the same Church of

[1] Martene, *de Ant. Eccles. Rit.* I. IV. Art. 12, ordo 21 (p. 597, Rotomagi). Scudamore gives the date as above, p. 617.

[2] This elevation of the Chalice seems to be a modified form of the elevation at "Qui pridie," but prolonged through the words of consecration.

Paris, a Constitution of William, Bishop of that diocese, seems to refer to the above order.

"Præcipitur, quod in celebratione Missarum, quando Corpus Christi elevatur, in ipsa elevatione, vel paulo ante, campana pulsetur, sicut alias fuit statutum, ut sic mentes fidelium ad orationem excitentur[1]."

The mention of bell-ringing is generally added in the accounts of this elevation. As the Canon of the Mass was said inaudibly, it was necessary, especially for those distant from, or out of sight of, the priest, for some such pronounced signal to be made.

The 13th century has special interest in relation to this new feature in the ritual of the Mass, on account of the formal promulgation of the doctrine of Transubstantiation in A.D. 1215.

It is related that Cardinal Guido, when he visited Cologne in A.D 1208 as papal legate to support the claims of the Emperor Otto IV., introduced there the custom that, when the Host was elevated, all the people, at the sound of a bell, should pray for pardon, and remain prostrate until the consecration of the cup. Thus in the early 13th century the custom had found its way into Germany, and was confirmed by the authority of Rome[2].

Sala (in his notes on Bona) quotes the following passage from a General Chapter of the Cistercian Order

[1] Mansi, xxii. p. 768.
[2] Cæsarius Heisterbacensis, *Historia*, ix. 51.

in A.D. 1215, the year of the Lateran decree: "Ut consecratione peracta Hostia elevaretur." He adds the comment:

"Quod antea factum fuisse non constat, nulla enim hujus mentio in libro Usuum Cisterciensium c. 53, ubi esse debuerat, cum ibi de consecratione disseratur[1]"

In the following year, A D. 1216, Pope Honorius III., in a letter to the Bishops of Ireland, decrees that at the elevation the people should reverently bow, the same honour being due when the Sacrament was carried to the sick. This was confirmed in the Decretals of Gregory IX.

"Sacerdos quilibet frequenter doceat plebem suam, ut, cum in celebratione elevatur hostia salutaris, quilibet reverenter inclinet, idem faciens cum ipsam portat presbyter ad infirmum[2]."

An interesting illustration to Englishmen is found in two letters of Ivo, Bishop of Chartres (Carnotensis), in the early years of the same (13th) century. In the first letter he writes to Matilda, Queen of England, pleading poverty, and begging for a gift of vestments for the Church at Chartres. The Queen responded

---

[1] Bona, L. ii. c. 13, § 2, p 284, n 7. In the same passage (note 4) Sala states that this new order in A.D. 1215 was given *shortly after* ("non multo post") the former order, which did not name the elevation after consecration. This points to the rise of the later ceremony about that date

[2] Honorius, *Ep ad Prælatos Hiberniæ*, Mansi, xxii. p 1100. For the reverence due when carrying the Sacrament to the sick, see *Constit Odonis*, A D. 1197, Mansi, xxii p 678

favourably, and in a second letter Ivo thanks her for her gift, not of vestments but of bells, and reminds her that her memory will be perpetuated among them by their use, whenever the Host is consecrated[1]. This points to the use of the large Church bells at the consecration, and, although no elevation is named, we know that from this time onward the completion of the consecration was marked by elevation, and by bell-ringing, both in the church tower and at the altar.

We can therefore assign the rise of this new ceremony, with a tolerable amount of certainty, to the end of the 11th century, while an accession of importance marked the epoch when Transubstantiation passed into a formal dogma.

It must, however, be remembered that at first the avowed object of this elevation was that of quickening devotion and stirring to prayer, although the express purpose of calling forth immediate adoration soon followed.

William, Bishop of Paris, in A.D. 1204, ordered the ringing of a bell at the elevation to stir up the minds of the faithful " to prayer." Cardinal Guido in A.D. 1208

---

[1] Ivo Carnot. *Epist.* 107, 142, Migne, *P.L.* clxii. pp. 125, 148, "Nec leviter est æstimanda talis memoria .quando illa singularis hostia, pro nobis redimendis in ara crucis oblata, per novi sacerdotii ministros in Domini mensa quotidie consecratur." Ivo has first said that the sound of the bells at certain hours would awake the Queen's memory, and then adds the above words. Presumably therefore the bells were also used at the consecration.

made the same order at Cologne that the people might then "pray for pardon." Walter de Cantelupe, Bishop of Worcester, in A.D. 1240, orders the bell to be rung "that thereby the devotion of the dull-minded (*torpentium*) may be roused, and the love of others more strongly kindled[1]."

But in the *Lay Folks' Mass Book* (13th century) the people are bidden, when the bell rings at the elevation, to do reverence to Christ's own presence, and to pray, "Welcome, Lord, in form of brede," and at about the same date genuflexion and adoration are expressly enjoined[2].

As early as 1197 the Constitutions of Odo of Paris direct the laity, when the reserved Host ("Corpus Domini") is carried by, to "bend the knee as to their Lord and Creator, and with folded hands to pray until it has passed[3]."

Again, in A.D. 1217, the Constitutions of Richard Poore, Bishop of Sarum, direct genuflexion at the elevation.

"Moneantur laici quod reverenter se habeant in consecratione Eucharistiæ et flectant genua maxime in tempore illo quando post elevationem Eucharistiæ hostia sacra dimittitur[4]."

The same direction appears almost verbatim in

[1] See pp. 104, 132.
[2] *Lay Folks' Mass Book*, pp. 38 f., 283 f.
[3] Mansi, xxii. p. 678.
[4] Mansi, xxii. p. 1119.

several other English Councils and Constitutions. See Additional Note, p. 131.

We can thus trace how the earlier purpose of elevation, namely to stimulate prayer and devotion, passed, under the growing influence of the belief in Transubstantiation, into that of giving a signal for the most profound reverence and adoration directed to the Sacrament of the Lord's Body and Blood.

The history, which we have traced, impressed itself upon the service-books from the 13th century onward. The rubrics, with few exceptions, distinguish between the earlier and more moderate elevation before consecration, and the later and more pronounced elevation which was avowedly to be seen by the people

This distinction is made in all the English uses except that of York, where "*Hic elevet hostiam*" occurs at "Qui pridie," but no higher lifting up after consecration is named[1]. The rest of the English Missals give plain directions for both elevations, and invariably mark the contrast in degree. The former is limited by the words *contra pectus, parum ab altari, paululum, sumat sursum*: the latter is to be *alcius, super frontem, ut videatur ab omnibus*.

---

[1] Yet the York *Horæ* appear to assume it by giving prayers "At the elevation of our Lord," and it finds a place in one MS. at Sidney Sussex Coll. Camb., which Canon Simmons designates "a fancy revision of the York Use according to Sarum." *Lay Folks' Mass Book*, p. 283

The following conspectus will illustrate this contrast:

Sarum, 13th century	Before "Qui pridie"	*Hic elevet hostiam contra pectus*
	After "Hoc est enim"	*Hic elevet alcius corpus ut videatur ab omnibus.*
Sarum, 14th century	Before "Qui pridie"	*Hic elevet hostiam parum ab altari.*
	After "Hoc est enim"	*Hic elevet hostiam ut videatur.*
	Before "Qui pridie"	*Hic elevet hostiam.*
Sarum, later form, and Bangor	Before "Tibi gratias agens"	*Elevet paululum.*
	After "Hoc est enim"	*Elevet eam super frontem ut possit a populo videri.*
Hereford	Before "Qui pridie"	*Hic sumat sursum hostiam.*
	After "Hoc est enim"	*Tunc elevet Corpus Christi in altum ut videatur ab omnibus*[1].

Thus all the English service-books, with the possible exception of the York use which notices only the earlier elevation of the Host at the words "Qui pridie," confirm the evidence which we have adduced, by marking the adoption, not later than the 13th century, of this new post-consecration ceremony.

The evidence of foreign services is very similar. A Dominican Missal of the 13th century has the rubric *aliquantulum elevet* at "Qui pridie," but *ipsam elevet* as soon as the Host is consecrated[2].

[1] *Tracts on the Mass*, pp. 11, 223 Maskell, *Anc. Lit.*, pp. 132 f.
[2] *Tracts on the Mass*, p. 80.

The Charterhouse and Carmelite Missals, *Alphabetum Sacerdotum*, and *Indutus Planeta*, all of the 16th century and representing the services of France and Italy, agree in giving the later and larger elevation after consecration, and generally direct that the Host should be made visible to the people. It is also noticeable that only moderate acts of reverence on the part of the priest are directed. Thus in the Charterhouse Canon:— "parum geniculat": "Post elevationem...reverenter inclinat sed non genuflectit" In the Carmelite:— "reverenter inclinans sine genuflexione" In the *Indutus Planeta*:—"adorato corpore Christi cum mediocri inclinatione[1]."

In the Coutances Missal (A.D. 1557), which gives one use in Northern France at the time of the Council of Trent, when the Pian Missal was being prepared, the earlier elevation has disappeared, being displaced by the later and larger elevation which was after consecration and for adoration (*in altum ut visum ab omnibus adoretur*). Yet only moderate bowing is ordered (*inclinet caput devote adorans*)[2].

But in Burckard's *Ordo Missæ* of 1502, which is thought by some to have papal authority[3] and represents the Roman use, we note a distinct advance. The lesser elevation is (as at Coutances) displaced by the greater (*elevat in altum quantum commode potest*

---

[1] *Ib.* pp. 45, 101, 186, 244. [2] *Tracts on the Mass*, p. 62.
[3] Addis and Arnold, *Dict.* s.v Rubrics.

hostiam), and distinct prostration (*usque in terram genuflexus*) is ordered, with adoration by both priest and people. We also find here the order that the minister is to lift up the chasuble "Ne ipsum celebrantem impediat in extensione brachiorum[1]."

Burckard's *Ordo* distinctly influenced the final Pian revision (A.D. 1570), in which a yet more elaborate ceremonial appears. Thus in the rubrics of the Canon itself we find immediately after "Hoc est enim,"—*statim hostiam consecratam genuflexus adorat, surgit, ostendit populo, iterum adorat*. Further, in the *Ritus celebrandi Missam* (A.D. 1570) the priest is ordered after "Hoc est enim" to kneel and adore, then standing erect to raise the host on high, and, with eyes fixed upon it, reverently to show it to be adored by the people. The server is also directed to lift the chasuble (*planeta*) lest it should hinder the celebrant in raising his arms at the elevation. The correspondence with Burckard, whose rubrics represent the most advanced ceremonial which we have traced, is thus evident in the Pian Order of the Mass, while, as we shall notice later on, this advance is less marked in all our genuine English Uses, up to the reign of Queen Mary.

(ii) *Elevation of the Chalice.*

We have now traced the evidence for the elevation of the Host, and pass on to notice the corresponding

[1] *Tracts on the Mass*, p. 156.

ritual at the consecration of the Chalice. And here we find the enquiry more complicated, partly because of the greater variation of place at which the elevation occurs, partly because it is sometimes absent altogether. Further complication arises from the facts that the words "Hæc quotiescunque feceritis..." (which are used in the English Prayer Book at the consecration of *both bread and wine*), are (with one exception) never[1] used in the pre-Reformation service-books at the consecration of the Bread, but of the Wine alone; and that the elevation of the chalice takes place, with a somewhat bewildering variation, *before, during*, and (in the Roman Use) *after* the recital of those words.

It is worthy of notice that, with few exceptions[2], the words are not, as we might expect, *Hoc quotiescunque...* (τοῦτο ποιεῖτε) but *Hæc quotiescunque...*the plural being used so as to refer to the benediction of both bread and wine. If this be so, they refer not to the consecration of the chalice only, as might at first sight appear, but to the whole action of the memorial which we celebrate in the consecration of both elements.

This view is adopted by W. Durandus in his *Rationale* (A.D. 1386). After minutely describing the ceremonial at the blessing of the chalice, he says of the

[1] I only know of one exception, the Mozarabic Missal, to which we possibly owe the double use of the words in our own service. See p. 145 f.

[2] The Sarum Missal (14th cent.) and the Mozarabic Missal read *HOC*. *Tracts on the Mass*, p. 11. Cf. p. 134 f. below.

words *Hoc quotiescunque*, "Hæc clausula, quia consecrationem tam corporalis (*sic*) quam sanguinis respicit, post depositum calicem debet dici[1]." His argument is that the words, since they refer to both Host and Chalice, are not fitly accompanied by the elevation of the Chalice alone, which should be replaced before they are pronounced Nevertheless it will be seen that in England and France the elevation of the Chalice sometimes takes place at these words. In the *Book of Common Prayer*, the singular "This" has been restored, and the words are repeated for each element, and the same restoration appears in the Mozarabic Canon, where again the words occur at each consecration. This variation in both the form and use of these words has added not a little complication to this part of our enquiry.

The ceremony of elevating the Chalice immediately after consecration has neither been so general nor so marked as that of the Host. It is wholly absent in some uses, and *extreme* elevation is rarely ordered.

This may have arisen from two causes. (1) The Bread may have been regarded as representing the two species, for, when the material views of Transubstantiation arose, and the Cup was denied to the laity, it was distinctly taught that either species contained the whole Body and Blood of Christ. (2) The fear of spilling the wine led to greater caution in directing

[1] *Rationale*, L. iv. c. 42, § 30.

any manual acts with the Chalice. Thus Sala, in his notes on Bona, after saying that with a view to visibility the Host was by some turned "hinc et inde," cites a German writer, Vincentius Grunez (early 15th century), to show that, while the Chalice was elevated in many Churches, yet in some it was not lifted *above the head*, lest the wine should be spilled. The passage is as follows:

"Secundum consuetudinem, inquit, multarum Ecclesiarum Calix elevatur alii...non elevant Calicem ultra caput, quod credo propter periculum et negligentiam evitandam esse inventum. Unde contigit, quod quidam sacerdos, cum ..Calicem supra caput levaret, et ex irregulari devotione motus se cum Calice et Sanguine Christi signare per modum Crucis supra caput vellet, Sanguinem Christi supra proprium caput fudit."

Sala adds that, in order to avoid such an unseemly result, it is enough to raise the Chalice *circa caput*, i e. not *ultra caput*. Yet in the later Sarum Canon extreme elevation is allowed,—"usque ad pectus *vel ultra caput.*"

But even this slight elevation of the Cup was not *universal* after consecration. In the 13th century Thomas Aquinas seems to have been ignorant of any such ceremony, and D. Soto (16th century), in his commentary on the *Sentences* of P. Lombard, attributes his silence to the fact that the ceremony was of later origin ("fortasse tempore sancti Thomæ mos ille nondum inceperat") He adds that Alexander of Hales (13th century), Bonaventura's teacher, speaks only of the elevation of the Body, and states that in the Missals of the Carthusian Order, to a branch of which (the *Prædicati*) he himself belonged, this elevation is not found. His reasons for this are the same as those given above, namely, the presence in the Host of the substance of both Body and Blood, and the physical risk of any extreme elevation of a cup containing wine[1].

It must, however, be noted that a slight elevation of the Cup is alluded to in the Carthusian statutes of the 12th century (see p. 103), according to which the Host also is elevated so as to be visible to the people[2].

Soto further remarks that some of the religious orders, whose rule was *not* to elevate the cup, disregarded the custom of their order because the secular clergy had adopted this later elevation ("Sed ne ab Ecclesiis Sæcularium dissideant illum (sc. calicem) elevant").

There would also appear to be a slight confusion in the terms employed, and an elevation of more moderate extent may not have been regarded by some writers as being technically "elevation" at all. That is to say, there may have been a slight "lifting up" even where no "elevation" of the Cup is expressly named, the technical "elevation" being regarded by some as "a

[1] D. Soto, *In Sententias*, iv. Dist. 13, Qu. 2, Art. 5, p. 591, "Quod ergo ad elevationem calicis attinet, veritas est quod mos ipsum elevandi non est antiquus." Soto, a Spaniard, was Charles V.'s "first theologian at the Council of Trent," and formulated the decrees from the decisions which had been passed.

[2] Martene, *de Ant. Eccles Rit.* I. iv. Art. 12, Ord. 21, pp. 597–8

question of inches." For instance Sala quotes from a Roman Missal dated 1507, of which he says, "signanter... ne verbum quidem legitur de elevatione Calicis post consecrationem." Yet the rubrics for the Cup do direct a *moderate* elevation *during*, though not expressly *after*, consecration: "Calicem accipit...et *parum elevat* dicens, 'Accipiens hunc'...Item *elevans* dicit, 'Accipite et bibite'...deinde *deposito Calice* dicit, 'In Mei commemorationem facietis[1].'" Again, in the quotation on p. 78 from the Council of Würzburg, a lifting up and holding "ante pectus" is not regarded strictly as "elevation"—"non *elevent* eam sed *ante pectus detineant*." This is contrasted with the showing to the people which follows—"tunc *elevet* eam decenter, *ita ut possit videri*."

We now propose to give a conspectus of the evidence for the elevation of the Cup in the English and in other service-books, in order to exhibit more clearly the character of the elevation and the varying times at which it was made.

Sarum, 13th century.

At "Simili modo,"   "*parumper elevet.*"
At "Hic est...facietis,"   "*elevet contra pectus.*"

Here the elevation commences with the recital of the Institution, and is continued to its close, but only moderate elevation is enjoined.

[1] Bona, ii. c. 13, n. 8, p. 285. This elevation, it is true, *commences before* the consecration, but *is continued during* it.

Sarum, 14th century.

At "Simili modo,"   (no mention).
At "Hic est...in remissionem
  peccatorum,"   "*parumper elevet.*"
Before "Hoc quotiescunque,"   the cup is replaced.

Here a moderate elevation takes place during the actual words of consecration, but the elevation ceases before the words "Do this in remembrance of Me[1]"

Sarum, later form (Burntisland Ed.), and Bangor.

At "Simili modo,"   "*teneat inter manus suas.*"
At "Hic est...peccatorum,"   "*Elevet parumper ita dicens.*"
At "Hæc quotiescunque,"   "*Hic elevet calicem usque ad pectus vel ultra caput, dicens*[2]."

Here the elevation commences with the recital, increases in intensity, and reaches its climax at the words "Do this in remembrance of Me," being lifted (in some cases) above the head.

York (in which no elevation of the Host is named).

At "Simili modo,"   "*teneat inter manus suas.*"
At "Hæc quotiescunque,"   "*Hic elevet calicem usque ad caput, dicens.*"

Here the elevation, at least in a pronounced form, is deferred until the words "Do this in remembrance of Me."

---

[1] Cf. Durandus (quoted p. 113), who states this to be the correct ritual.

[2] The Sarum Consuetudinary (14th cent.) gives similar directions, but some MSS. omit the further elevation at "Hoc quotiescunque." W. H. Frere, *Use of Sarum*, I. p. 81.

Hereford.

At "Simili modo,"	"*teneat eum per medium.*"
At "Hic est enim calix,"	"*Elevet aliquantulum calicem et aperte dicat.*"
Before "Hæc quotiescunque,"	"*Tum elevet calicem in altum ut videatur ab omnibus, et statim reponat...et cooperiendo eum dicat*, 'Hæc quotiescunque.'"

The elevation of the Cup after consecration is here to be such that the people may see it, and it ceases before the words "Do this" &c., as in the 14th century Sarum Use[1].

We proceed to compare the usage in foreign service-books.

Carthusian Constitutions (said to be of 12th century)[2].

At "Simili modo,"	"*elevat parum.*"
At "Benedixit" to end of words of Institution,	"*elevat parum.*"

Dominican Missal (13th cent., France)[3].

At "Simili modo,"	"*ipsum modicum elevet.*"
At "Benedixit,"	"*iterum levet et teneat eum sicut prius.*"
At "Hæc quotiescunque,"	"*reponat et operiat corporali.*"

[1] A MS. of the 14th century, preserved in the Library of University College, Oxford, differs in some points from the printed edition of 1502. Thus a slight elevation of the Cup occurs at "Accipite et bibite," and the elevation *in altum* is altogether absent. See *Hereford Missal*, edited by W. G. Henderson, p. 128.

[2] Martene, *De Ant. Eccl Rit.* I. iv. 12, Ordo 21. Cf. *Tracts on the Mass*, p. 101.

[3] *Tracts on the Mass*, p. 81.

Indutus Planeta (early 16th cent., France)[1].

At "Simili modo,"	"*parum elevat.*"
At "Accipite et bibite" to end of words of Institution,	"*iterato elevans.*"

Alphabetum Sacerdotum (late 15th or early 16th cent., France)

No elevation named at "Simili modo" or at "Hic est enim calix."

At and during "Hæc quotiescunque...facietis,"	"*Hic levet calicem, et levando dicat.*"

Coutances (1557, France).

At "Simili modo,"	"*accipiat eum ambabus manibus.*"
At and during "Hæc quotiescunque,"	"*Hic elevet calicem dicens*"

Burckard (1502, Rome).

At "Simili modo,"	"*illum aliquantulum elevat.*"
At "Hic est calix,"	"*accipit ambabus manibus*"
At "Hæc quotiescunque,"	"*Reponit calicem super corporalia dicens.*"

Roman (1570).

At "Simili modo,"	"*ambabus manibus accipit calicem*"
At "Hic enim est...peccatorum,"	"*tenet illum parum elevatum.*"
At "Hæc quotiescunque,"	"*Deponit calicem...dicens.*"
After words of Institution,	"*Genuflexus adorat, surgit, ostendit populo iterum adorat.*"

[1] *Ib* p. 187.

To these may be added the rubric of a Carmelite Missal (dated 1532) in which the words "Hic est... peccatorum" are followed by this rubric: "*eum (calicem) reverenter adoret, moxque resumente calicem... aliquantulum levet ut tamen adstantibus apparere possit, nisi consuetudo patriæ aliud habeat, dicendo* Hæc quotiescunque...[1]." The rubric is singular both in regard to the elevation, *though slight, being such as to make the cup visible to the people,* and in the condition laid down that the custom of the country is to be followed. This gives additional support to the opinion that there was a considerable variety of use, which is difficult to analyse, as to the manner and time of elevating the cup.

In the Ambrosian Missal published A.D. 1560, ten years before the Pian Missal, the rubric before "Hæc quotiescunque" is *Levet, et in elevatione dicat.* The elevation at "Qui pridie" and "Simili modo" has disappeared, and at "Hoc est enim corpus" is very guarded—*Levet discrete, et ostendat populo per morulam*; no elevation of the Cup occurring till that just mentioned[2].

This variety of use seems to show that there was no intimate connexion between the ceremony of elevation and the words "Do this in remembrance of Me," which followed the consecration of the Cup. In

[1] *Tracts on the Mass,* p. 244.
[2] Martene, I c. iv. Art. xii Ord. 3 (p. 476)

recent times the ceremony has been closely associated with these words, yet there are but uncertain liturgical grounds for so doing, and we have observed no evidence that the elevation which sometimes accompanied them was intended to suggest a sacrificial meaning.

The Roman Use, dating from A.D. 1570, has no elevation at these words. The Cup is replaced before they are recited, having been slightly elevated at the consecration, and is afterwards shown to the people.

In other Uses, partly English and partly Continental, the elevation is sometimes completed before the words "Do this in remembrance of Me" are pronounced, sometimes an earlier elevation is continued during them. In only a few of the services which have been examined is the elevation definitely limited to these words. They are the York, Carmelite (A.D. 1532), Coutances (A.D. 1557), and Ambrosian (A.D. 1560) Uses, and that described in the *Alphabetum Sacerdotum* (15th or 16th cent.). In the Mozarabic Canon the elevation is directed between the words "Hoc est Corpus," &c. ("Hic est calix," &c.), and the words "Quotiescunque manducaveritis (Quotiescunque biberitis), hoc facite in Meam commemorationem." See p. 134

The evidence adduced seems to justify the following conclusions. A considerable variety of use existed as to the time and manner of elevating the Cup. This elevation was probably adopted at a later date than that of the Host, and when adopted was at first only a moderate elevation[1], which, however, developed in the 15th and 16th centuries into a ceremony almost identical with the elevation of the Host.

This raises the important question whether any account can be given which explains this special treatment of one element, or whether we must seek some different interpretation for the elevation of the Cup, especially when made at the words "Hæc quotiescunque," which appear to apply to both Bread and Wine.

Durandus, who gives reasons with great detail for the elevation of the Host, evidently regards both elevations as having one significance, but seems to treat that of the Cup more lightly, simply adding "licet sanguis videri non possit, superflua non est." See p. 159.

Several considerations help to explain the special phenomena of the elevation of the Cup. The consecrated Bread was itself actually visible, the wine in the Cup was not so, and in an elevation *to be seen by the people* this circumstance might well lead to that of the Cup being regarded with less attention and

[1] The words used in our English rubrics were—in Sarum, "ante pectus," "parumper," "aliquantulum," but in York, "usque ad caput," Hereford, "in altum ut videatur ab omnibus," and later Sarum, "usque ad pectus vel ultra caput." In foreign rubrics we find "parum," "modicum," "elevet" and in the Mozarabic "elevetur" of both Bread and Cup · but in the Roman Missal of 1570, "genuflexus, adorat, surgit, ostendit populo iterum adorat."

considered to be of minor importance. The fact that the Host had already been seen by all may partly account for the lesser elevation of the Cup.

We have also seen (pp. 113 f.) that great caution was exercised in lifting up the Cup, lest the wine should accidentally be spilled, and that a more moderate lifting up (e.g. "circa caput") was recommended[1]. These considerations,—the priority of the elevation of the Host, the invisibility of the actual wine, and the danger of spilling it,—seem sufficiently to account for the more moderate elevation of the Cup, and consequently its lesser ritual importance.

Yet it may reasonably be asked whether so slight an elevation could have for its object the showing of the Cup to the people, and this at least suggests the enquiry whether any other purpose was intended. But no other purpose is suggested by the rubrics, and a higher elevation of the Cup is ordered in the Bangor, York, and later Sarum Uses, while in that of Hereford it is expressly enjoined to be so that the people may see. In the Carmelite Missal (p. 120) the elevation, though slight, is to be distinctly visible.

At the beginning of the 16th century the purpose was certainly understood in England to be the same for both elements. In the *Rationale* or "Book of

---

[1] This caution seems to be reflected in Burckard's *Ordo Missæ* (1507)—"elevat eum *quantum commode possit*, illum populo ostendens adorandum."

Ceremonies," prepared in Henry VIII.'s reign, it is stated that the Cup is lifted up "that the people with all reverence and honour may worship the same, and also to signify thereby...Christ's exaltation upon the cross for our redemption." See p. 160[1].

There is therefore no indication of any distinction of significance, but the less prominent lifting up in some rites, and its total omission in others, point to a relative diminution of ritual importance, fully accounted for by the peculiar circumstances of the case. Both convenience and caution led to a less striking ceremonial, such as the rubrics indicate, in the elevation of the Cup.

(5) *Elevation at the Communion of the people.*

This late elevation, introduced in the 16th century at the Communion of the people in the Church of Rome, has already been considered in relation to the Eastern, Mozarabic, and "Omnis honor et gloria" elevations. See pp. 59—62.

DEVELOPMENT OF CEREMONIAL AFTER A.D. 1215.

This period in Church History, which witnessed the rise of a new ceremony intended to express a newly

[1] In the Carthusian Ordinary (c. 1500) the elevation of the Cup during the words "Hæc quotiescunque" is said to be for the purpose of signifying its specially sacred character: "Elevat calicem parum alcius *ad distinguendum sacrum a non sacro*." Cf. Hildebert Cænom p. 77. *Tracts on the Mass*, p. 101

formulated doctrine of the Real Presence, was also marked by a rapid development of the outward signs of reverence paid to the consecrated elements. To the great majority of worshippers the climax of the Mass came to be, not the act of communion, but the elevation and adoration of the Host. An extreme elaboration of ceremonial followed. Everything was done that the genius of the later Roman Church for splendid ritual could devise, so as to present a solemn and impressive spectacle of which the lifting up of the consecrated wafer was made the central and absorbing act.

The greatest care was now taken to accentuate the exact moment when the tremendous mystery of transubstantiation took place. Even the older ceremony of elevation at "Qui pridie" and "Simili modo" was cautiously modified, or even abolished, lest what was still "the creature" should receive the worship only due to "the Creator[1]." Nor was this unreasonable, when it is remembered that the Canon of the Mass was recited inaudibly, and in a language "not understanded of the people."

As a consequence the crisis of consecration was emphatically proclaimed, not only by the elevation of the Host high above the head, but also by the ringing of bells both in Sanctuary and Church-tower, the kindling and lifting up of lights, and the lowliest

[1] Cf. p. 133, "ne pro creatore creatura. veneretur." *Synod of Exeter*.

prostration of priest and people, even those in the houses and fields being exhorted to mark by timely reverence the event which the tolling of the Church bell announced[1].

Mr Edmund Bishop points out that much which is now regarded as a natural accompaniment of the service is of comparatively recent date.

"For instance," he says, "we do not realise at once how much of added and imposing ceremonial is involved in the addition, in the 12th and 13th centuries, of the single act of the elevation of the Host and Chalice, with its accompanying lights and torches, censings, bell-ringings, and genuflexions"

These, we are told, should be regarded as later introductions when we try "to figure to ourselves the true and unadulterated Roman ceremonial of the Mass[2]."

Nor was this all. The practice of reservation for the purpose of communion was seriously affected by this development of doctrine, and by the ritual that accompanied it. The practice of sending the consecrated elements to those not present in Church is mentioned as customary in the middle of the 2nd

---

[1] It is customary in Malta to fire salutes at the time of elevation from the forts of St Elmo and St Angelo. Canon Simmons relates (*Lay Folks' Mass Book*, p. 282 n.) how two English officers were court-martialled for refusing to carry out this order from conscientious scruples. Access to the forts is now allowed to the Maltese for this purpose.

[2] *Genius of the Roman Rite*, p. 10

century[1]. To prevent abuse this custom was restricted, from the 4th century onwards, to the purpose of communicating the sick[2], and later on, in the 9th century, a tabernacle was provided on the altar in which it was reserved[3]. But in the 11th century, when the controversy on Transubstantiation arose, and that doctrine became generally recognised, minute directions began to be given as to the kind of reverence which was everywhere and always due to the reserved Sacrament. Genuflexion and adoration were required, not only at the elevation, but on passing an altar where the elements were reserved. The manner of carrying the Sacrament to the sick was carefully laid down, and the same honour was to be given to it when carried by in the road, as at the supreme moment of consecration in the church. To ensure this, the priest bearing the Sacrament was to be robed in a surplice, and accompanied by lamp, cross, and bell[4].

The festival of *Corpus Christi* is a part of the same development. It was first ordered to be observed in 1264, with the desire "to stem the heresy of Berengarius, and to promote the doctrine of Transubstantiation," and the procession of *Corpus Christi* was introduced in 1320, for the special honour and adoration of the consecrated Host[5].

[1] Justin M. *Apol* I lxvii.   [2] *Dict. Chr Ant.*, s. v. Reservation.
[3] Mansi, xiv. p. 891.   [4] Wilkins, I pp. 579, 637, 657
[5] Mansi, xxiii. p. 1077, and xxv. p 649.

At a much later date the service of "Benediction with the Sacrament" marked a further development in the use and adoration of the reserved Host. This rite was unknown until the 16th century, and includes the exposition of the Host for the express purpose of blessing the people.

Among the new marks of outward reverence which characterised this period of ritual progress, none was more striking and significant than that of genuflexion, which was the natural complement of elevation, as that ceremony was now interpreted. Speaking generally, it was at this time that the pronounced act of bending the knee (*genua flecti*) took the place of the more simple bowing of the head (*inclinare caput*). This became the recognised response of the people to the elevation by the priest.

At an earlier period it was sometimes customary not to *kneel*, but to *stand* at the elevation A Dominican Missal of the 13th century orders the Host to be so lifted up as to be visible to those who stood at the further end of the Church (*retro stantibus apparere*)[1]. And Hugh Patshull, Bishop of Lichfield, in 1240, directs the people to stand—"adoret stando[2]." Passages have been already quoted (p. 53) in which the words "adstantes" and "circumstantes" are used of the people present at the consecration.

[1] *Tracts on the Mass*, p. 80.
[2] Dugdale, *Mon. Anglic.* viii. 1259, London, 1817-30. See Rock, *Ch. of our Fathers*, iv. p 181.

This was a survival of the old idea that kneeling was the attitude of penitence, and that standing best expressed the feeling of Eucharistic reverence. In the 16th century J. S. Durantus condemns those who taught "quod in elevatione Corporis Jesu Christi non debent fideles assurgere, nec ei reverentiam exhibere[1]." In another passage he says: " At hodie—proh Dei et hominum fidem !—non desunt qui, dum SS. Eucharistia ostenditur, stantes et operto capite eam intueantur[2]." It is the due reverence, not the particular attitude, that he insists upon.

It is a fact of some interest that in England, while the laity are frequently bidden *genua flecti* at the consecration, it was never enjoined that the priest at the altar should genuflect in the Creed or in the Canon. There is an exception in the Hereford Use, where at the words *Et incarnatus est* of the Nicene Creed the rubric runs "*et fiet genuflexio*" (Rom "*Hic genuflectitur*"). Mr Frere adds another exception at Exeter, "where much English ceremonial was deliberately given up in favour of Roman ceremonial in the middle of the 14th century[3]." This also was in the Creed and is deliberately stated to be a following of Rome. Even in Mary's reign, when the adoration of the Host is first expressly enacted in the English Canon, genuflexion is not named[4]

[1] *De Rit Eccles. Cathol* ii. p. 567 f   [2] For ref. see p. 105.
[3] *Religious Ceremonial*, pp. 123, 293.
[4] " Et capite inclinato illam adoret." See *Lay Folks' Mass Book*, p 283.

But for the laity not only is genuflexion enjoined, but in a canon of a Synod at Exeter (A.D. 1287) a distinction between a careless bowing and genuflexion is expressly made. This may be an instance of the same tendency in that diocese to adopt Roman ceremonial which has just been named. The words are — "ut in elevatione corporis Christi non irreverenter se inclinent, sed genua flectant, et Creatorem suum adorent omni devotione et reverentia[1]."

In the Church of Rome genuflexion at this point of the service is made the subject of elaborate directions. Thus in the *Directorium Divinorum Officiorum* (16th century) of Ludov. Ciconiolanus the writer laments that some priests only do slight reverence after consecration ("parum tanto domino inclinari"), and insists that only the sick and aged can be excused from the most profound acts of reverence. For all others— "genuflectiones post consecrationem profundissime fieri condecet." In the *Rubricæ Generales* of the Roman Missals the priest's ceremonial is extremely full and precise[2].

[1] Wilkins, *Concil* ii p. 132.
[2] *Tracts on the Mass*, p 215. *Miss. Rom Rubricæ General.* xvii

ADDITIONAL NOTE A.

EXTRACTS FROM THE CANONS OF ENGLISH COUNCILS
OF THE 12TH AND 13TH CENTURIES

In Appendix F to the *Report of the Royal Commission on Ecclesiastical Discipline* (1906) a number of extracts are given from the Canons of English Councils of the 13th century which show how fully this ceremony of elevation after consecration had taken hold of the English Church. As might be expected, the purpose seems to lean sometimes to the earlier and simpler stirring of devotion, at other times to the fully developed worship of the Host. The quotations there given refer also to the reverence due to the reserved Sacrament, during the time of reservation, and specially when carried to the sick. Although this subject is not strictly within the scope of our enquiry, yet we have noticed it as illustrating the marked increase of ceremonial which the development of doctrine inevitably produced. Such ceremonies, especially in combination, have a value which is relative to the doctrine involved[1]. A few of these extracts are now given.

The Council of Oxford, A.D. 1222. "Frequenter moneantur laici, ut ubicunque videant corpus Domini deferri, statim genua flectant tanquam Creatori et Redemptori suo, et junctis manibus quousque transient, orent

[1] "A series of many practices, each of which would separately come in the first or second class" (i.e. be not open to serious objection), "may, in combination, produce a result open to very grave objection." *Report of Royal Com. on Eccles. Discipline*, p 16.

humiliter, et hoc maxime fiat tempore consecrationis in elevatione hostiæ, quum panis in verum corpus Christi transformatur, &c.[1]"

The Constitutions of Alexander de Stavenby, Bishop of Coventry, A D. 1237. "Unde precipimus, quod in elevatione eucharistiæ *quando ultimo elevatur et magis in altum*, tunc primo sonet campanella, quæ sit quasi modica tuba denuncians adventum judicis, &c [2]"

The words italicised point to the distinction between the earlier and lesser elevation at *Qui pridie* and *Simili modo*, and the later and more extreme elevation after consecration We have seen that the still later elevation at *Omnis honor*. and at the close of the Canon is never enjoined in the English rite. The expression "Quando *ultimo* elevatur" would not have been applicable to the Roman rite, pp. 94 f.

The Constitutions of Walter de Cantelupe, Bishop of Worcester, A.D. 1240. "Cum autem in celebratione missæ corpus Domini per manus sacerdotum in altum erigitur, campanella pulsetur, ut per hoc devotio torpentium excitetur, ac aliorum charitas fortius excitetur[3]." The same Constitutions direct that a lamp should burn day and night before the reserved Sacrament.

The Statutes of Norwich, A.D. 1257. "Sacerdos vero quilibet frequenter doceat plebem suam, ut cum in celebratione missarum elevatur hostia salutaris se reverenter inclinet[4]."

The Constitutions of Archbishop Peckham at Lambeth, A D. 1281. "In elevatione vero ipsius corporis Domini

---

[1] Wilkins, *Concil* 1. p. 594 [2] *Ib.* p. 640.
[3] *Ib.* p. 667. [4] *Ib.* p. 732.

pulsetur campana in uno latere, ut populares, quibus celebrationi missarum non vacat quotidie interesse, ubicunque fuerint, seu in agris, seu in domibus, flectant genua[1]."

The Synod of Exeter, A D 1287. "Quia vero per hæc verba 'Hoc est enim corpus meum,' et non per alia, panis transubstantiatur in corpus Christi, prius hostiam non levet sacerdos, donec ipsa plene protulerit verba, ne pro creatore creatura a populo veneretur."

"Hostia autem ita levetur in altum, ut a fidelibus circumstantibus valeat intueri, per hoc enim fidelium devotio excitatur, et fidei meritum suscipiat incrementum. Parochiani vero solicite exhortentur, ut in elevatione corporis Christi non irreverenter se inclinent, sed genua flectant, et creatorem suum adorent omni devotione et reverentia; ad quod per campanellæ pulsationem primitus excitentur, et in elevatione ter tangatur campana major[2]"

ADDITIONAL NOTE B

THE CONSECRATION IN THE MOZARABIC MISSAL

(*See also pp.* 36*f.*, 96*f for this Missal.*)

The form of consecration in the Mozarabic Missal has a peculiar character, showing a distinct relationship, on the one hand, to the early Eastern Liturgies, and, on the other, to the latest and most Western,—the Communion Office of the Church of England.

[1] *Ib.* ii p 52
[2] *Ib.* ii. p. 132. *Report of Royal Commission*, Vol iv. pp. 71 f

A new feature is here added to the history of elevation, in the fact that both the Bread and the Cup are elevated after the words of consecration, and before the words, "Quotiescunque manducaveritis, hoc facite, &c.," and "Quotiescunque biberitis, hoc facite, &c." This form is peculiar to the Mozarabic service. The consecration is as follows:—

"Dominus noster Jesus Christus in qua nocte tradebatur accepit panem, et gratias agens benedixit, ac fregit, deditque discipulis suis dicens. accipite et manducate. HOC EST CORPUS MEUM QUOD PRO VOBIS TRADETUR *Hic elevetur corpus.* Quotiescunque manducaveritis, hoc facite in meam + commemorationem Similiter et calicem postquam cœnavit dicens, HIC EST CALIX NOVI TESTAMENTI IN MEO SANGUINE, QUI PRO VOBIS ET PRO MULTIS EFFUNDETUR IN REMISSIONEM PECCATORUM. *Hic elevetur calix coopertus cum filiola.* Quotiescunque biberitis, hoc facite in meam + commemorationem...R Chorus Amen Quotiescunque manducaveritis panem hunc, et calicem istum biberitis, mortem Domini annunciabitis donec veniat...[1]"

For the later elevation before the Creed and Lord's Prayer see pp. 96 f.

Several points of interest call for notice. It will be seen that the words "Do this in remembrance of Me" occur twice, at both the consecrations: and accordingly the original form "*hoc* facite" (τοῦτο ποιεῖτε) takes the place of the later "*hæc* quotiescunque feceritis," which is only recited in other Latin services after the consecration of the Cup, and apparently refers to the whole consecration.

The Mozarabic Liturgy is thus linked with several Eastern and with the Anglican group of Liturgies. In some Eastern Offices the words only occur once, as in the

[1] Martene, I. iv. 12, Ordo 2, p. 462.

WESTERN LITURGIES

Latin Offices, but in others they are repeated for both the Bread and the Wine and this is so in all the members of the Anglican group.

In the Eastern Liturgies, however, there are considerable variations in the use of this phrase, these variations being on the whole what might be expected from a study of the several forms which the story of the Institution takes in the New Testament.

The words τοῦτο ποιεῖτε κ τ.λ. do not occur either in St Matthew's or St Mark's account, in St Luke's and St Paul's they vary as follows:—

St Luke.	St Paul.
After the Bread only,	After the Bread,
τοῦτο ποιεῖτε εἰς τὴν ἐμὴν ἀνάμνησιν	τοῦτο ποιεῖτε εἰς τὴν ἐμὴν ἀνάμνησιν.
	After the Cup,
	τοῦτο ποιεῖτε ὁσάκις ἂν πίνητε εἰς τὴν ἐμὴν ἀνάμνησιν.

In no account are they found after the Cup only.

The Eastern services present instances of the form given by St Matthew and St Mark, i.e. where they omit the words entirely, and also of St Paul, i.e. where the words are used after both parts of the consecration. I have not seen any corresponding to St Luke's form, i e. where they are used after the Bread only.

The following instances will illustrate these variations. In the *Apostolic Constitutions*, and in the Liturgies of St James and St Mark (all of the Syrian group of services), the words occur for the Cup only, as in the Latin Missal. The same form is followed in the Liturgies of St Basil and of the Armenians (in the Byzantine group), and in the Abyssinian Liturgy. It is noticeable, however, that τοῦτο never becomes ταῦτα *These do not follow any of the New Testament narratives.*

In the Coptic and Ethiopic Liturgies, and in the Nestorian (Persian) Liturgy, the words are said for both Bread and Cup, as in the narrative of St Paul.

In the Liturgy of St Chrysostom, both in that of the 9th century and in the present form, there is a total absence of these words, an absence which we have noted in the narratives of St Matthew and St Mark.

The Mozarabic Use therefore, like our own, reproduces in the West a form which is found in some Eastern Liturgies, but which differs from that found in all other Western rites.

But there is another feature in the Mozarabic Use (not reproduced, so far as I have observed, in any Western rite except in that of Milan), which has also an Eastern counterpart, and which can hardly have had an independent origin.

At the close of the benediction of the Cup the choir respond, "Amen. As often as ye shall eat this bread and drink that cup, ye shall proclaim (annunciabitis) the Lord's death till He come." This use of St Paul's words in 1 Cor. xi. 26 is found in several of the Eastern Liturgies, not in most cases as a response[1], but as the closing words of consecration[2], and often with the addition "and confess my resurrection and taking up (ἀνάληψιν) until I come."

---

[1] The Syrian Liturgy of St James, and the Liturgies of the Coptic and Abyssinian Jacobite Church, give the words as a response by the people, as in the Mozarabic rite.

[2] We give the form found in the *Apostolical Constitutions* Τοῦτο ποιεῖτε εἰς τὴν ἐμὴν ἀνάμνησιν ὁσάκις γὰρ ἂν ἐσθίητε τὸν ἄρτον τοῦτον

This use is found in the various forms of the Syrian rite, in the Egyptian Liturgies (except the Ethiopic), and in the Byzantine Liturgy of St Basil, but not in the Nestorian or Ethiopic Liturgy, or in that of St Chrysostom. It is also adopted in the Ambrosian Liturgy of Milan, but not in the form of a response as in the Mozarabic Missal[1].

The close resemblance between the Mozarabic words of Institution and our own has led some to the opinion that Cranmer in A.D. 1549 directly adopted the Mozarabic form This theory gains support from a further resemblance in the Baptismal Office[2] But it seems more probable that he was following the Brandenburg-Nuremberg service of A.D. 1533, especially as the people's response in the Mozarabic Use is not followed, and the actual words correspond more closely with the Lutheran than with the Spanish formula[3]. It is also to be noted that the same form of words came into England in another connexion, namely in Cranmer's version of the Catechism of Justus Jonas where the origin is undoubtedly Lutheran. It was published in 1548 under the Archbishop's oversight.

Each of the two ceremonies of elevation found in the Mozarabic Missal has its counterpart in other Western Missals, and probably serves the same purpose. We have found no evidence which tends to separate the elevation

καὶ τὸ ποτήριον τοῦτο πίνητε τὸν θάνατον τὸν ἐμὸν καταγγέλλετε ἄχρις ἂν ἔλθω. By the change to τὸν ἐμόν the words are made a continuation of the words of Institution.

[1] Martene, i p 476, c. iv. Art. xii. Ord. 3.

[2] The series of short petitions commencing "O merciful God, grant that the old Adam in this child may be so buried &c" are based upon a form found in the Mozarabic rite

[3] Gasquet, *Edw. VI. and B C. P.*, pp. 444 f

after consecration in the Mozarabic Liturgy from that which arose in the Western Church in the 12th or 13th century. The position of both ceremonies is identically the same. Hardly less obvious is the correspondence between the Mozarabic elevation before the Creed and Lord's Prayer, and that of the Western Canon at "Omnis honor et gloria." But the late post-consecration ceremony does not seem to have attained to the same prominence in the Mozarabic as in the other Western rites, in which the earlier elevation at "Omnis honor et gloria" became attenuated and regarded as the *elevatio minor*. In the Mozarabic rite the latter seems to have retained its original importance as an encouragement to immediate communion.

CHAPTER III.

THE RATIONALE OF ELEVATION.

THE interpretation put upon this ceremony has varied very widely, and at some points of the service it is not easy to place its purpose and meaning beyond dispute We proceed to consider how far the various opinions that have been held may be applied to the several forms of elevation which have prevailed in the Church.

It was noted at the outset of this enquiry that the act may signify one or other of two distinct things.

(1) It may partake of the nature of the heave-offering, and so declare in action that the things lifted up belong to God, and are thus presented to Him. It may also be a memorial (אׇזְכָּרָה, $\mu\nu\eta\mu\delta\sigma\nu\nu o\nu$), i e something by which we plead with God on the ground of His covenant with man. Or again, some regard it as a symbolical act expressing our desire that our worship may be brought into relation with the heavenly realities and so partake of their virtue and effect.

All these ideas are based on elevation as a *Godward* act.

(2) It may be employed for the simple purpose of displaying the symbols and pledges of our redemption to the congregation before communion. In this aspect it may combine both invitation and warning. Or it may be regarded as representing in dramatic form some central truth, either to evoke more generally the devotion of the people, or to summon them to an adoration definitely directed to the consecrated gifts

In all these the appeal is *to the mind of man.*

In seeking to differentiate these two aspects we must give the greater weight to the expositions of those who wrote when a particular ceremony was of recent origin, and had not crystallized into a more formal act of ritual of which the meaning was dim and dubious. After that process has taken place, there is a danger of reading new ideas and doctrines into old forms, as when Roman writers interpret the early Greek elevation in the light of modern theological developments. What we want is the fresh thought born of true devotion interpreting a living speaking ceremony, not a new theory seeking the support of older ritual, and unconsciously putting into the ceremony what historically it never meant.

New interpretations of such a ritual action as this may arise, may by frequent repetition win approval, and ultimately receive authoritative sanction from some new rubric or canon. There is a danger, while this process is going on, of leaning upon interpretations which are merely conjectures, and have no real support in the actual history. Our endeavour must be to ascertain the spiritual truths which were originally intended, or have been commonly accepted, in one section or another of the Church.

In the two earlier acts of elevation (at the Offertory and at the "Qui pridie") all the evidence points to the conclusion that a God-ward act of devotion was intended. The elevation is not primarily a presentation to man, although indirectly all such acts tend to stimulate devotion.

(a) Where elevation has accompanied the Offertory, there can be no question as to the meaning always and everywhere assigned to it. Whether the ritual be that of the *Prothesis* in which "the gifts" are prepared in a side-chapel for the "Great Entrance," or that performed by the Deacon or Priest at the Holy Table, the same spiritual act of oblation and dedication to God's service is intended. In earlier times, the simple act of placing the gifts upon the Holy Table sufficed to express this presentation of God's own gifts to Him; but in later times, and especially in the Western Church, a more definite act of "lifting up" was enjoined.

There is very little express testimony as to the meaning of the Offertory-elevation, probably because its general adoption was late, and its significance beyond dispute. Yet it must not be forgotten (as we have already noted) that the words of some of the prayers *before* consecration seem to refer to the whole action of the service, and that the "offering of *the Host*" (p. 72) is so named even when the only offering has been that at the Offertory or First Oblation. This probably points to a time when the whole service was regarded as an *Eucharistia*, or "sacrifice of praise and thanksgiving," and before the exact definitions as to time and result of consecration were severely pressed The dedication of gifts to God's service included the whole idea of sacrifice, so far as the service allowed it. See pp 146 f.

(*b*) The next act of elevation (again common to both Eastern and Western services) was that which was gradually developed out of the recital of the words of Institution, and took place at the "Qui pridie" and "Simili modo." This elevation is closely connected with the "manual acts," which in primitive use were doubtless intended to represent as closely as possible our Lord's own action when He instituted this Sacrament.

There can be little or no doubt that by these "manual acts" it was intended to celebrate the "perpetual memory" of our Lord's passion, so as to be seen by those who were about to communicate. But the custom, which arose in the East, of withholding the consecration from the view of the worshippers, inevitably obscured the primitive purpose of the manual acts, and to this hiding of the central act of commemoration we may possibly trace the rise of the Eastern ceremony of elevation at the words τὰ ἅγια τοῖς ἁγίοις

But another purpose came to be recognised in these acts, which also found expression in the elevation at "Qui pridie" and "Simili modo." Some of the Eastern Liturgies, as we have already noticed, adopted the tradition that our Lord "showed the Bread and Wine to the Father" (see pp. 19, 22). The reference to this thought is rare, and the mention of elevation in this connexion both rare and late. When it appears, it is an Eucharistic extension of the manual acts in accordance with this early but not universal opinion, the presentation of the Bread and Wine to the Father being regarded as part of our Lord's act of "giving thanks" (εὐχαριστήσας).

In the West the evidence is much more clear, although the Eastern extension of the words is not adopted. The earliest mention of it in the *Micrologus* (11th century)[1] suggests a presentation for the purpose of benediction. It is said of the Bread, "panis in manus accipitur, et antequam reponatur in altare benedicitur": and more expressly of the Cup, "item et calix elevatus ante depositionem benedicitur." This is done moreover in imitation of what our Lord did: "Nam et Dominus in Evangelio utrumque legitur

[1] *Micrologus*, c. 15. See pp. 74 f

benedixisse antequam dimitteret e manibus." In the *Micrologus* therefore the manual act of elevation is regarded as the proper accompaniment of a bestowal of blessing upon the elements.

In the important passage quoted from Honorius of Autun (12th century), a similar purpose is named, and the same reference is made to our Lord's example. He regards the elevation as an extension of the act of taking the elements into the hands ("exemplo Domini"), and the object in view is expressly described,—"ut sit Deo acceptum"—the sacrifices of Abel, Abraham, and Melchisedek being named as in the Canon itself[1].

Hildebert of Tours, in his *Carmen de Officiis Missæ*, does not expressly formulate this intention, but he too lays stress on the act of "taking" and "lifting up" ("Sumitur et sumptum tollit utraque manu") being continued until the recital of the actual words of Christ is completed. But in his view the chief purpose of exhibiting the elements is that they are now a more excellent food than any common food ("communibus escis altior et quiddam majus[2]"). We have therefore three important witnesses as to the purpose of the "Qui pridie" and "Simili modo" elevations in the 11th and 12th centuries, and the God-ward aspect of the ceremony is clearly recognised in them, although in Hildebert the purpose of invitation to the people also appears.

[1] p. 76. [2] p. 77.

THE RATIONALE OF ELEVATION

We have seen how the history of this particular elevation becomes obscured in the 12th and 13th centuries by the necessity of dealing with it in relation to the newly adopted elevation after consecration. Thus the history of the "Qui pridie" elevation brings into clear relief the extreme sharpness of distinction that arose between the proper kinds of reverence due to the elements before and after consecration. The call for some such distinction will appeal to most devout and reverent minds. Even dangerous exaggeration must not lead us to ignore the distinction altogether. After consecration the Bread and Wine have a relation to the Body and Blood of our Lord which did not exist before that act was completed. The gifts presented at the Offertory are separated to some sacred use, but it is the consecrated Bread and Wine that are in such sense the Body and the Blood, that "we receiving them" are partakers of that holy food. The dignity and honour of our Lord are brought into closest relation to them, and they are "holy things for holy men[1]."

Yet the evidence of the early Liturgies does not warrant so severely marked a distinction as that which our enquiry shows to have been made in the 13th and 14th centuries. We have already considered (p. 72) how in the earlier parts of the service the elements are spoken of in the most solemn terms as the offering

[1] See Waterland, *Doct. of Eucharist*, c vi. p. 90 (Clarendon Press, 1896). He speaks of this as "relative holiness."

made to God. In the Gallican Liturgy they were, at the "Procession of the Oblation," already designated as the Body and Blood of Christ[1].

This was regarded by some as a serious confusion, and in the case of the elevation before consecration great care and caution were observed to prevent it. To anticipate the reverence due at the "Second Oblation" was to commit a kind of idolatry.

It is probably a truer view, and one which accords with this language of the Liturgies, if we regard the Eucharistic service as a whole in the light of a λογική λατρεία, and the presence of Christ as not limited by the conditions of time and space. Bishop John Wordsworth (speaking of the outward devotion practised at the "Great Entrance" of the Eastern Church) says, "Its best defence is surely that the Ancient Church did not limit the presence of Christ to one moment in the service, but beheld Him throughout ministering to His people" And again, "The voice of the Church is 'It is no longer common bread but Eucharist, consisting of two parts, an earthly and a heavenly.'...On the other hand the Church shrank from fixing the moment of this mystery...She did not define that up to a certain definite instant common bread was there, and then at a given minute and in a given space, which could be pointed at with the finger, or announced with

---

[1] Duchesne, *Christian Worship*, p. 204.

the ringing of a bell...the divine power was brought into the earthly forms[1]."

Such a view seems fully to accord with the spirit of the Liturgies in their earlier forms. They enjoin the most careful and intense reverence in dealing with elements now dedicated to so solemn and sacred a use, yet are wholly devoid of any suggestion of worship or adoration directed towards the elements themselves either before or after consecration. Later and more material conceptions of the Lord's presence in the Sacrament compelled a tribute of worship which is severely defined as to time, place, and motion. But in the earlier Christian ideals of an Eucharistic service, the consecration of the elements and our Lord's presence in Communion seem to have been conceived on deeper and more spiritual lines.

If our reading of the evidence be correct, both the elevations before consecration were meant to be of the nature of presentations of our gifts to God. At the Offertory the action was more general, involving the presentation of all gifts, and not merely of the bread and wine for communion, for God's acceptance and service. At the recital of our Lord's words of Institution the presentation was more special, for only the bread and wine were presented, and that with the purpose of blessing and so consecrating them to a specially holy use.

[1] *Holy Communion*, pp. 88, 110.

The loss of the primitive ceremony of "fraction," which followed the "taking" of the Bread, may be connected with the loss of the original intention that the actual celebration should be visible to all. That this openness was part of the primitive ceremonial can hardly be doubted when we remember that the earliest name by which the Lord's Supper was known was the "Breaking of Bread[1]." For this name would not have been given, if that significant act had not been visible in the earliest Christian services. Yet we have seen that open fraction "before the people" disappeared at this point of the Liturgy, and that the thought of presentation to God became dominant, while the presentation to the people was reserved in both Eastern and Western rites until the consecration was complete. For the restoration of the primitive custom in the Anglican Church, see pp. 175 f., 178 f.

(c) When we turn to the post-consecration forms of elevation, whether immediately following the consecration or at the close of the Canon, we find the most general interpretation to have been that which connects them with the crucifixion and burial of our Lord. It also appears that an appeal is thus made to the imagination and devout feelings of the people, who are thereby roused to deeper devotion, and to prepare themselves

[1] Acts ii 42, 46, ἦσαν δὲ προσκαρτεροῦντες τῇ κλάσει τοῦ ἄρτου Cf. xx. 7, 11. Cf. also St Luke xxiv. 35, ἐγνώσθη αὐτοῖς ἐν τῇ κλάσει τοῦ ἄρτου.

III] THE RATIONALE OF ELEVATION 149

for communion. The elevation presented a vivid picture of the passion of Christ, and in some writers the various actions of the priest and his assistant minister are taken to represent in dramatic form the principal incidents of that solemn hour.

In itself such a rehearsal of the passion might be regarded as a representation *before God* of our Lord's atoning sacrifice. But, so far as the evidence before us may be taken as a guide, this idea is not found either in Eastern or Western writers, save in one important passage ascribed to Bonaventura. Nor do the rubrics or accompanying words of the services suggest this thought with any distinctness.

It will be more convenient to treat of the Eastern and Mozarabic elevations, together with the Western elevation at " Omnis honor et gloria," apart from the elevation of the Bread and Wine immediately after consecration, as the former have several features in common, and are of distinctly earlier date.

There seems to be no doubt that both the Eastern and Mozarabic elevations after the Canon were for the purpose of exhibiting to the people the consecrated elements before communion.

(i) St Germanus (p 49) interprets the Greek elevation of the Death upon the cross and of the Resurrection, and a Syrian writing of the 8th century, ascribed to St John of Damascus, bears witness to the same interpretation. The passage is as follows—

Εἶτα ὑψοῦται ἐν ταῖς χερσὶ τοῦ ἱερέως ὡς ἐπὶ σταυροῦ καὶ διαδίδοται κλώμενον, καὶ οὕτως ἐν ἡμῖν θάπτεται καὶ συναφθαρτίζει ἡμᾶς[1].

The intention indicated in these words would seem to be to represent to men's minds the sacrifice which they commemorated, and thus to prepare them for the salutary reception of the broken Bread, in partaking of which Christ's Body was received and "buried" in them.

It is needless to repeat here what has been said on Archdeacon Freeman's view, or to review the reasons which led us to the conclusion that the elevation, accompanied by the words τὰ ἅγια τοῖς ἁγίοις, was for the purpose of inviting the congregation to such consecration of themselves as would make them meet partakers of the consecrated gifts.

(ii) The purpose of the Mozarabic elevation after the Canon is equally clear. It was in order to display the consecrated bread to the people—*ut videatur a populo*. It was moreover followed by the recital by the people of the Nicene Creed, which links closely the Mozarabic with the Eastern elevation, that being also followed by the people's response in the form of an open confession of faith. Thus the Eastern and Mozarabic forms have a common purpose, and in all probability a common origin. This is important as

---

[1] *De Corp. et Sang.*, Migne, *P.G.* xcv. c. 409.

bearing upon the meaning of the elevation at "Omnis honor et gloria" which we shall next consider.

(iii) No mention of *purpose* occurs in the *Ordines Romani* in which the elevation at "Omnis honor et gloria" first appears. But Amalarius (9th cent.) compares the action of the priest and deacon with that of Nicodemus and Joseph in their care for the Sacred Body of our Lord, and in the same century Rabanus Maurus interprets this elevation as suggestive of (*insinuat*) the Crucifixion (see p. 89).

The same exhibitive intention is named by John of Avranches about the year 1070. He says—"(Exprimitur) per elevationem de altari hostiæ depositio Christi de cruce, per depositionem iterum in altari sepultura Christi." It is noteworthy that the comments on this passage[1] contrast the elevation at "omnis honor, &c." with the more recent Roman elevation, but make no distinction as to meaning.

We have already seen that Ivo of Chartres (12th cent.) connects the act of elevation with the ceremony of crossing the chalice, and with our Lord's own words, "I, if I be lifted up, will draw all men unto me[2]." He thus associates the elevation with the attractive power of "Christ crucified" over the hearts of men, and anticipates the more explicit statements as to the intention of this ceremony. The witness of Hugo de S. Victore, which is of the same age and country, refers

[1] Migne, *P.L.* cxlvii. c. 36, 78. [2] St John xii. 32. See p. 90.

to the same elevation, and expresses the same symbolical ideas. See p. 91.

We have direct testimony to the purpose of the Roman elevations in the *Expositio Missæ* ascribed to Bonaventura (12th cent.) by the Vatican editors of his works in 1588, but rejected by more recent critics as not a genuine work of the great schoolman. Yet its inclusion in his works warrants us in regarding it as a writing of some value, and as evidence of current views in the 16th century, and the work itself doubtless represents those of an earlier date.

The following is the *rationale* given of the elevation at " omnis honor ":

"Quod autem corpus Christi supra calicem in ipsa hora levatur, et cum ipso calix signatur, per hoc intelligi datur, quod mors a Christo superatur, vita reparatur, et gloria datur, et de hoc patet in verbis canonis *per ipsum et cum ipso et in ipso*. Nota quod in hoc loco Missa correspondet omnibus horis canonicis, quia omnia quæ Christus passus est in ea representantur et memorantur." (The events of the passion are here enumerated in relation to the canonical hours.) "Sequitur *per omnia sæcula sæculorum* quod alta voce pronunciatur, et Corpus Domini super calicem et cum calice levatur, per quod intelligi datur, quod tristitia Apostolorum de passione Domini ab eorum cordibus ipso reviviscente fugabatur, et gaudium resurrectionis annunciabatur."

The passage is fanciful, as when it is said that in the Mass are represented "all things that Christ suffered," these things being then assigned to the seven canonical hours. But it is none the less valuable as showing what was the general conception of the scope and aim of this part of the service. The crosses and subsequent elevation are explained as a mystical exhibition of the sufferings and triumph of our Lord. The writer is a strong exponent of the sacrificial aspect of elevation, but there is no hint of such a meaning here, for the sacrificial presentation has taken place, as he believes, at the earlier elevation, i e. immediately after consecration (see p. 163 f.).

In the earlier Missals, where both "the crosses" and the subsequent elevation are named, no rubrics occur which throw light upon the meaning and purpose of these ceremonies. But in the 16th century clear indications appear that they were then intended to attract the attention of the people to the great mystery which was now being celebrated.

We have seen that in the Missals of the Churches of Coutances, Sens, Nevers, and Lyons, the elevation at the close of the Canon was to be seen by the people, and that distinct adoration was in some places enjoined, e g. at Lyons, Cordova, and in the Premonstratensian Canons. The later order to adore was thus grafted on to the much earlier ceremony of elevation at this point of the service (see p. 94).

In England, although there is no mention of elevation at the close of the Canon, as in the foreign Missals, yet we have noted (pp. 94—96) how popular custom led to the ceremony of "the crosses" at "per ipsum, &c." being regarded as one at which people might see the Host, if they had failed to do so at the greater elevation. In this way our English services bear indirect witness to a series of actions with which the Canon closed, and which were so executed as to be visible to the people.

It is hard to believe that the Mozarabic elevation *after* the Canon is not closely connected in origin and meaning with that which marks the close of the normal Canon of the Western Church. The position, though not identical, is very similar, and we have marked the variable position of the Western elevation, which sometimes occurred in the Lord's Prayer, or even as late as the *Embolismus*. These variations are of later date, but are indications that the ceremony was not held to have any *essential* connexion with any particular phrase in the service. See pp. 92 f.

Moreover the Mozarabic elevation links the elevation at "omnis honor, &c." with that of the Eastern Liturgies, and it seems probable that in all three cases the elevation was originally intended to exhibit to the people the elements now prepared for their communion.

Mr Chambers[1] in his *Divine Worship* states that on some coins of Chilperic and Charibert in the 6th century, and of Lothaire in the 10th century, a round Host is exhibited above a Chalice. If this be so, it forms an interesting confirmation of the early date of this double elevation at the close of the Canon

[1] Late Recorder of Salisbury. *Divine Worship*, p. 367.

in the West, and of its being an elevation which was so familiar a sight as to be recognised by those who used the currency. But the Keeper of Coins at the British Museum (who has kindly allowed me to consult him) does not confirm the statement. Such coins have the chalice surmounted by the cross, but not by the Host, so far as he has observed them.

In the same work Mr Chambers gives the following *rationale* of the elevation at " omnis honor, &c."—" The ritual reason for elevation was that the food which had been consecrated was so very excellent and superior that it ought to be treated with signs of all reverence[1]." This corresponds with several of the passages quoted above, and with the general conclusion that the ceremony was intended to present to the people a vivid representation of the benefits wrought by the passion of our Lord.

It must be allowed that the original purpose of the elevation at "omnis honor" cannot be decided with the same certainty as that of the Eastern and Mozarabic elevations after the Canon. The direct evidence that it was intended to display the elements to the people is of much later date than the origin of the ceremony, and in some cases is connected with the comparatively recent purpose of adoration. Moreover the words which most frequently accompany it are expressive of Eucharistic thought:—" Per ipsum

[1] *Ib.* p. 368

et cum ipso et in ipso est Tibi Deo Patri omnipotenti, in unitate Spiritus Sancti, omnis honor et gloria."

Accordingly Archdeacon Freeman and Mr W. H. Frere hold that the ceremony was a natural lifting up of the elements to God. The former says, "The idea is that the Body and Blood of Christ, mysteriously exhibited here on earth, may by contact with the Heavenly Altar, on which Christ Himself is ever mysteriously presented...be fulfilled with *Celestial* efficacy...It designs to place the Things consecrated on earth on a par with the glorious Reality in Heaven. It seeks, on behalf of all the mystic Sacrificial Gifts, the grace inherent in the original, meritorious, ever-abiding Sacrifice." He also connects it with the Lord's Prayer which follows "for right reception and for freedom from all evil[1]." This, it will be remembered, agrees with the same writer's interpretation of the Eastern elevation. See pp. 38 f.

Mr Frere contrasts the intention of the elevation at "omnis honor" with the novel elevation after consecration. He says of the latter, "It therefore differed in intention as well as in position from the older and less conspicuous elevation which...was made at the close of the Canon, and was the natural God-ward action of offering[2]." The *exact* nature of the offering is not stated, but the words "Omnis honor et gloria"

[1] *Principles of Divine Serv.* pp. 176 f.
[2] *Relig. Ceremonial,* p. 94.

suggest an act of praise and thanksgiving similar to that contained in the first post-communion prayer of the English Prayer Book, which ends in words which are evidently taken from the close of the Canon.

This view, however, lacks external support, and it seems unlikely that in the Western service there should have been no ceremony for the purpose of showing the consecrated species to the people until the new Western elevation arose, especially as this was so carefully provided for in the Eastern and Mozarabic rites. The absence of any mention of this Eucharistic view by the author of the *Expositio Missæ* (see p. 152), when he expounds at length the meaning of the elevation and crosses, makes it improbable that it was the recognised interpretation, especially as he fully adopts a sacrificial view of the elevation after consecration.

On the whole it seems most probable that the object of the elevation at "omnis honor, &c." was the same as that of the Greek and Mozarabic elevations after the Canon and shortly before communion. This is the view adopted by Dr Wickham Legg[1], who says, " This showing of the Sacrament to the people, at the end of the Canon, is very ancient, far older than the elevation after *Hic est enim*, &c." And again: " It seems likely enough that at the beginning this elevation in the West, too" (i.e. as well as in the East), " was only an invitation to communion, taking place as it does

[1] *Tracts on the Mass*, p. 241.

immediately before the Lord's Prayer, which is the commencement of the preparation of the communicants."

(d) No such uncertainty obscures the purpose of the elevation after consecration. The cause which gave rise to its adoption by the Western Church, and its avowed intention, can be clearly traced. The development of the doctrine of Transubstantiation, and its condemnation by Berengarius, suggested the thought of a new elevation in the 11th or 12th century, which had been hitherto unknown in any Church of Christendom.

The formal promulgation of the doctrine in A.D. 1215 led to a rapid development of the ceremonies of which this novel elevation was the chief, and out of the purpose of stirring dull minds to more fervent devotion was shortly evolved that of claiming immediate and intense adoration.

This growing purpose has already been reviewed while tracing the growth of this form of elevation from the 12th century onwards. The passages which witness to its rise bear unequivocal witness to its purpose also. The Host is to be elevated so as to be seen by all. The time is marked as one at which pardon and grace are to be specially sought in prayer, and the moment of consecration becomes distinguished by an elaborate outburst of ceremonial action, calculated to arouse the feelings and impress the minds of the worshippers.

In the 13th century there is an advance in the direction of fully developed adoration. Durandus (A.D. 1296) illustrates the varied aspects of elevation which then prevailed in the five reasons which he gives for it. He is speaking of the elevation at the words *Hoc est enim corpus Meum*.

1. "Ut cuncti adstantes illud videant et petant quod proficit ad salutem." He quotes "Ego si exaltatus fuero a terra..."

2. "Ad notandum quod non est aliud dignum sacrificium, immo est super omnes hostias."

3. "Signat Christum verum panem, per prophetas in Scripturis exaltatum, qui ejus incarnationem prophetizabant...et hunc cibum fore cæteris excellentiorem."

4. "Significat resurrectionem"

5. "Hostia elevatur ut populus non præveniens consecrationem, sed ex hoc cognoscens illam factam esse, et Christum super altare venisse, reverenter ad terram prosternentur, juxta illud ad Phil. *In nomine Jesu omne genu flectatur*, et illum corde et ore adorent[1]."

Thus at the end of the 13th century the simpler idea of representing Christ lifted upon the cross has developed into the express purpose of evoking adoration at the moment when Christ has become present on the altar, that adoration being scrupulously guarded against before the consecration is complete. This exact

[1] *Rationale*, IV. c 41, § 51—53, p. 112.

measurement of time does not appear before the later view of the presence of Christ was developed.

The progress of development can be clearly traced in the evidence before us. From the 9th to the 12th century the elevation of Christ upon the cross, and the superior excellence of the Eucharistic food, are chiefly noticed. In the 13th century the purpose of stimulating devotion and rousing dull minds to livelier emotions, by the sight of what was now hailed as the true Body and Blood of our Lord, comes into view. Later on, immediate prostration and direct adoration are expressly directed for all in the presence of the consecrated Host.

Elevation is very fully explained in the *Rationale* of Henry VIII.'s reign, the ceremony referred to being that immediately following consecration.

"Which he lifteth up both that the people with all reverence and honour may worship the same, and also to signify thereby partly Christ's exaltation upon the cross for our redemption, which was figured by the serpent set up by Moses in the desert, and partly signifying that triumphant advancement and exaltation whereto God the Father because of His passion has exalted Him above all creatures, bidding the people to have it in remembrance as oft as they shall do the same[1]."

But while such adoration is expressly claimed as a Christian duty in the *Rationale*, which represents current opinion and custom, the English Missals lag

[1] *Rationale* or *Book of Ceremonies*, Collier, v. p. 117. Strype, *Eccles. Mem* I. P. ii. p. 424.

behind. High elevation for ostension to the people is there, and the bowing of the head is named in the Bangor Use, but there is no express incitement to adoration until the reign of Mary, when in A.D. 1554 a Sarum Missal contained the rubric "*Et capite inclinato illam (Hostiam) adoret.*" It is not unreasonable to say that this addition was made under Roman influence, while at the same time it must be fully conceded that a widespread opinion and use had already sanctioned it[1].

That the simpler view of the sacring still lingered on in some cases may be seen from the account of the chaplain's duties at St Paul's School, as laid down in the Statutes drawn up by Dean Colet.

"The Chapelyn. There shall be also in the scole a preste, that dayly as he can be disposed shall sing masse in the Chapel of the scole, and pray for the children to prosper in good life and good literature to the honor of God and our Lord Christ Jesu. At his masse when the bell in the scole shall knyll to sacringe, then all the children in the scole knelynge in their seats shall

[1] The Roman Missal of A.D. 1570 puts it still more strongly both in the rubrics and in the *Ritus Celebrandi* See p. 111 Blunt says (*Dict. of Theol.* s.v. Elevation). "But it is observable that no such rubric was ever introduced into the Anglican Liturgy, in which the direction was, 'Post hæc verba (of Institution) inclinet se sacerdos ad Hostiam et postea elevet eam supra frontem ut possit a populo videri,' and for the cup 'ad pectus vel ultra pectus, dicens *Hæc quotiescunque* ,'" with which he contrasts the Roman words "prolatis verbis consecrationis statim Hostiam genuflexus adoiat." The words for the cup in the Sarum Missal (Burntisland ed.) are "ad pectus *vel ultra caput.*" See *Lay Folks' Mass Book*, p. 283.

with lift upp handes pray in the time of sacringe. After the sacringe when the bell knylleth agayne, they shall sitt downe agayne to their bokes learninge[1]."

A special interest attaches itself to a passage in the Vatican edition of Bonaventura's writings, the full discussion of which has been reserved to the last, because of its unique character.

It is singular that in all the evidence now adduced there has been so little reference made to the God-ward aspect of elevation. We have seen that at the Offertory, and at the opening words of the Institution, this is the probable meaning of the lifting up. But these are pre-consecration ceremonies and do not concern the consecrated elements. We have also seen that in the 13th and 14th centuries this distinction between elevation before and after consecration was clearly and emphatically made.

That both Eastern and Western services contain many phrases which imply an oblation of the Bread and Wine after consecration needs no proof. Yet they are never accompanied by the act of elevation. The manual act of crossing abounds, and corresponding postures of reverence are enjoined, but the act of elevation, whenever performed after consecration, seems hardly ever to have been so explained. Neither Durandus nor Durantus suggests it, and the evidence as a whole points to a different idea, namely that of

[1] *Life of Colet* by S Knight, p. 306

displaying to the people the symbols of our redemption.

It is true that the elevation is sometimes only "contra pectus," but the case of the chalice, where precaution led to this lesser elevation, prevents the conclusion that, where the elevation was but slight, a different purpose was involved.

This makes the witness of Bonaventura all the more remarkable. He distinguishes between the two post-consecration elevations, explaining the later one after "the crossings" as a representation of Christ's passion and victory over death, while to the earlier form when the Host was shown to the people he attributes a distinctly sacrificial and God-ward significance. Of the latter he says,

"Nunc autem videndum est, quare in Missa sacerdos Corpus Dominicum in altum levat et fidelibus adstantibus ostendit. (1) Quarum prima et præcipua est ad gratiam Dei Patris, quam peccatis nostris perdimus, obtinendam. Solo enim peccato offenditur et irritatur, sicut dicit Psalmista, *Irritaverunt Deum inventionibus suis*. Sacerdos igitur elevat in altari Corpus Christi, quasi dicat 'O pater cœlestis, peccavimus, et Te ad iracundiam provocavimus. Sed nunc respice in faciem Christi filii Tui, quem Tibi præsentamus, et Te ab ira ad misericordiam provocamus....' (2) Ad impetrandum et obtinendum omne bonum ... (7) Ad ostendendam bonitatem Christi. Ecce quem totus mundus capere non potest, captivus noster est, ergo eum non dimittamus, nisi quod petimus prius obtineamus."

It seems, however, to be very doubtful whether the *Expositio Missæ* is a genuine work of Bonaventura It was reckoned to be his by the Vatican editors of his works in 1588—1599[1], but that was three centuries after his time. It is accordingly found in the edition published "Moguntiæ, 1609." But in the recent edition[2] it does not appear, and it is stated in the Preface to be probably spurious, Bonelli alone regarding the work as genuine.

This witness to the meaning of the elevation at the consecration is very remarkable, as thus combining the two ideas of elevation. On the forefront is placed the thought of the presentation of the elements to God, not merely as a pleading of the merits of Christ, but as a distinct offering of Christ to Him. Coupled with this is the thought of proclaiming to the people the greatness and goodness of God in the gift of His Son, and the fact of the presence, as "our captive," of Him whom "the whole world cannot contain."

Apart from this passage, only the elevations previous to consecration are spoken of as having a God-ward or sacrificial intention, while those which follow are intended to be seen by the people. But the words ascribed to Bonaventura at least suggest the thought that, to some, the twofold idea of elevation was present in the later Roman ceremony.

We have no reason to suppose that the elevation

[1] Bonaventura, *Opera*, T. vii. p. 78. Moguntiæ, 1609.
[2] "Ad Cleras Aquas (Quaracchi), 1882," vol. i. p. 19 and x. p. 22.

immediately after consecration in the Mozarabic Missal has an origin differing from that of the normal Western Canon, or that the purpose is other than that of exhibiting the elements to the people immediately after the consecration has been completed. It occurs in the case of both species between the formula of consecration and the words "Hæc quotiescunque &c." As in the other forms of the Western Canon, there is a later elevation before the Lord's Prayer, which is intended, like the Eastern elevation at τὰ ἅγια τοῖς ἁγίοις, to prepare the people for communion.

(e) The elevation of the Host at the communion of the people has been already sufficiently explained. It is of late origin, appearing first in the *Ritus Celebrandi Missam* of A.D. 1570, and bears a close resemblance to the Eastern elevation before communion. It is an exhibition of the consecrated element to the communicants immediately before reception, is accompanied by the words "Ecce Agnus Dei, Ecce qui tollit peccata mundi," and is never carried out except when there are communicants. The plain purpose seems to be that of exhibition before communion, but it is impossible to dissociate it from the avowed significance of the exhibition of the Host in the Church of Rome.

CHAPTER IV.

ELEVATION AND THE BOOK OF COMMON
PRAYER.

AT the Reformation the ceremony of elevation was regarded by the Reformers with peculiar suspicion. Bishop Ridley orders in his visitation of the diocese of London in 1550, "That no minister do counterfeit the Popish Mass" by "making any elevation of the Sacrament." Bishop Hooper repeats the same order[1].

Steps had already been taken before that year to put an end to this usage. The "Order of Communion, 1548" expressly left the ceremonies of the Mass unchanged, but provided a short office of Communion in English, which restored the Cup to the laity, and *forbade elevation* if a fresh consecration of wine were necessary.

The two rubrics which direct this should be

[1] Cardwell, *Doc. Ann.* i. p. 93. Cf. Hooper, *Later Writings*, p. 128, Parker Soc. "That none of you do counterfeit the popish mass in . *shewing the sacrament openly before the distribution of the same, or making any elevation thereof.*"

compared. "The time of the communion shall be immediately after that the Priest himself hath received the Sacrament, *without the varying of any other rite or ceremony in the Mass* (until other order shall be provided)...save that he shall bless and consecrate the biggest chalice or some fair and convenient cup or cups full of wine with some water put unto it." And at the close of the service the consecration of more wine, if needed, is provided for according to the old form, but without the words *Hæc quotiescunque*[1], and *without any levation or lifting up*. Elevation was therefore left at the main consecration in the Canon, but forbidden if there was a second consecration of wine, no further consecration of bread being provided.

In 1549 the "other order" referred to in 1548 was provided. Elevation was now wholly forbidden at the consecration. "These words before rehearsed are to be said, turning still to the Altar, *without any elevation, or shewing the Sacrament to the people.*" The only elevation left was the simple manual act of taking the bread and cup into the hands as directed in the rubrics. No breaking or laying on of the hand is mentioned, but a later rubric directs *fraction* for the convenience of distribution.

In 1552 the rubric forbidding elevation was removed. The reason for this, considering the whole temper and tendency of this revision, cannot have been to restore

[1] As not part of the essential words of consecration.

elevation, or leave it an open question. It was probably omitted, because all mention of manual acts was at the same time omitted, so that the prohibition to elevate was thought needless With this omission the history of elevation in relation to the Book of Common Prayer comes to a close. But several changes were subsequently made in 1662 which have an indirect bearing upon our subject, and illustrate the attitude of Anglican divines of the 17th century towards those conceptions of worship of which elevation is significant

It will be convenient now to summarise the successive changes made in the Anglican Office of Holy Communion at those points where elevation had been expressly named in the earlier service-books, and with this summary our investigation may fitly close.

In connexion with the various positions in which we have traced the rise and development of elevation, it is interesting to notice that every one of them is represented in our Anglican Office, although the accompanying ceremony is nowhere named.

This is obviously true of the Offertory, the manual acts and consecration, and the actual communion. But it is not generally recognised that one of the few phrases of the Canon of the Mass adopted in the Prayer of Consecration in 1549, and retained in a different position in all subsequent revisions, is the " Omnis honor et gloria," at which the earliest Western elevation took place. We place the passages together for the sake of comparison; slightly altering the order of words in 1549.

Sarum Canon.	Prayer of Consecration, 1549.
"Per † ipsum. et cum † ipso. et in † ipso	"By whom and with whom
est Tibi Deo Patri omnipotenti	be unto Thee, O Father almighty,
in unitate Spiritus sancti	in the unity of the Holy Ghost,
omnis honor et gloria.	all honour and glory
Per omnia sæcula sæculorum."	world without end."

The correspondence is nearly exact[1], and in both cases the Lord's Prayer immediately follows.

In subsequent revisions these words were retained, but the whole prayer of oblation was placed after the communion of the people. The retention of this venerable form of words, with which the Western Canon had for centuries closed, serves to mark the strongly Eucharistic intention of this prayer

We proceed to notice several other parts of the Anglican Office with which the ceremony of elevation had in the past been connected, and to estimate how far the thought underlying that ceremony is retained.

The Offertory.

The history of the "first oblation" in the English Prayer Book shows a characteristic alternation between a reasonable desire to retain so ancient a custom, and

[1] " et in ipso " is omitted.

a natural shrinking from anything that might, however unreasonably, be confused with the "sacrifices of Masses" condemned in Article XXXI. In 1549 the offerings of the people "unto the poor mennes boxe" were made immediately before "the Canon[1]," but there was no direction to place them upon the Holy Table, or to present them before God. In this particular Cranmer followed the mediæval service-books which did not provide for the larger oblation of gifts.

There was moreover a trace left of the old offerings of the bread and wine to be used for communion. The rubrics directed that each house should in course "offer every Sunday, at the tyme of the Offertory, the juste valour and price of the holy lofe"; and further that "some one at the least of that house in every parish" should receive the Holy Communion with the priest, communion without communicants being now forbidden, but no number yet specified

It was further enjoined in 1549 that the elements required for communion should be "set upon the altar" immediately before the Canon. No elevation was directed, and there was no formal oblation in words until after the recital of the Institution, when this form of oblation was used,—"We Thy humble servants do celebrate and make here before Thy divine Majesty,

---

[1] This name is once retained in 1549. See rubric in the Communion of the Sick, "*unto the end of the Canon.*"

IV] BOOK OF COMMON PRAYER 171

with these Thy holy gifts, the memorial which Thy Son hath willed us to make, having in remembrance, &c., &c."

There were no directions of any kind in A D. 1552 as to placing either the alms or the elements upon the Holy Table, and no words or acts of oblation are hinted at. Even the prohibition to elevate disappeared, probably because no manual acts of any kind were prescribed.

Matters remained in this condition until A.D. 1662. But there is evidence that early in the 17th century it became usual with some clergy to revive certain usages of 1549, and even of an earlier date. Among these was the oblation of the alms and of the elements at the Offertory[1].

Bishop Andrewes describes the priest as bringing the wafer-bread and wine to the Bishop, and then says, "These the bishop offers, in the name of the whole congregation, upon the altar. Then he offers into the basin for himself, and after him the whole congregation[2]." Here apparently the elements only are described as being *ministerially* "offered[2]."

On the other hand Bishop Wren in A.D. 1636 describes "the Holy Oblations" (by which he means the alms) as "received by the minister standing before the

[1] There is no hint of any post-consecration offering, but when Dr Oglethorp insisted upon elevating the bread before Queen Elizabeth, it was doubtless at the time of the "elevation of the Host," i.e. after consecration.

[2] *Minor Works*, p. 153.

table...and then by him so reverently presented before the Lord, and set upon the table till the service be ended." He makes no mention of an offering of the elements[1].

Bishop Cosin also, in his account of the English service in *Regni Angliæ Religio*, &c., distinctly mentions the custom of placing " upon the Altar or Lord's Table " the elements for consecration. And Prynne, in his *Canterbury's Doom*, charges Abp Laud with introducing a " *Credentia* or side-table " into his chapel, on which the bread and wine were first placed, and then the chaplains " being about to consecrate the elements " took them from the *Credentia* and " offered up the bread and wine thereat upon their knees, and then laid them on the altar[2]."

At the last revision some of these rubrically unauthorised restorations were adopted, while others found no recognition in the new rubrics. The rubrics then adopted enjoined the reverent placing of " the alms for the poor and other devotions," and also of the bread and wine, upon the Holy Table. The order of A.D. 1549 was not exactly followed, for whereas at that date the elements only were to be placed on the Holy Table, now both alms and elements are to be placed there at the Offertory. Also, the alms and " other devotions of the people " are to be " reverently

[1] *Notes on the Book of Common Prayer*, Minor Works, p. 153.
[2] Cosin's *Works*, IV. p. 358. *Cant. Doom*, p. 63.

brought" to the Priest, "who shall humbly present and place (them) upon the holy Table," but no express direction (probably for reasons of caution) is given to "humbly present" the Bread and Wine, but only that they are to be placed with the other offerings at the time of oblation. It is to be remembered moreover that in the Prayer for the Church Militant both "alms and oblations" are "offered," but whether the bread and wine are included under the term "oblations" is at least uncertain[1].

There seems to have been the intention, tempered with great caution, to restore in this manner the primitive offering to God of all the people's gifts for His service. There is no express direction to elevate, beyond what the words "humbly present and place upon the Holy Table" may reasonably suggest, but the spiritual act of dedicating our gifts to God by laying them before Him was restored. It is the Offertory-Oblation.

The Consecration.

At this point much greater caution was observed both in the independent action of Caroline divines, and in the final revision of A.D. 1662, when the action of the priest at the Holy Table was much more carefully regulated.

[1] See Bp Dowden's Article in the *Journal of Theological Studies*, April, 1900

"Any elevation, or showing the Sacrament to the people," had been expressly forbidden in A.D. 1549, and the manual acts at consecration limited to the simple ceremony of "taking the bread" and "taking the cup" into the priest's hands. Fraction was not restored at the recital of the Institution[1], nor yet the act of blessing by laying the hand upon the elements.

We may be sure that the men who in A.D. 1552 removed all mention of those most primitive acts, which were ordered in A.D. 1549, had no intention of restoring elevation when they omitted the rubric which forbade it.

Matters were left in this position until the Restoration, but it was felt, not only by Anglicans but also by Puritans, that such an absence of all ceremonial

[1] A subsequent fraction is enjoined in one of the closing rubrics of 1549, not ceremonial, but for the purpose of distribution. The bread is to be "unleavened and round, as it was afore, but without all manner of print, and something more larger and thicker than it was, so that it may be aptly divided in divers pieces and every one shall be divided in two pieces, at the least, or more, by the discretion of the minister, and so distributed." This is clearly not the κλάσις but the μελισμός (see p. 21). The insistence on dividing each piece of bread probably points to the symbolism of the one body and many members declared by St Paul to be signified by the "one loaf" distributed among the many communicants. This symbolism of the fraction is probably better supported by primitive language than the reference, which has for centuries been almost universally adopted, to our Lord's Body broken for us upon the cross. Yet this interpretation, hallowed by venerable use, and sanctioned by the teaching of the New Testament, will retain its hold on Christian thought as presenting one of the most treasured views of Holy Communion.

acts robbed the celebration of Holy Communion of what made it a much more exact and more helpful commemoration, by failing to reproduce what our blessed Lord Himself *both said and did*. There is little wonder that clergymen supplied the lack at their own discretion, and it was probably this feeling that prompted the Puritan request at the Savoy Conference, which will presently be noticed.

Among the ceremonies not enjoined by the rubrics, yet openly practised during the reigns of James I. and Charles I., were the manual acts at consecration. Bishop Cosin in his notes on the Book of Common Prayer (2nd series, dating from Charles I.'s reign) speaks of these manual acts as "still observed among us[1]." What they were may be gathered from a passage in his *Regni Angliae Religio Catholica* (A.D. 1652), where he thus describes this part of the service:

"Deinde, sese erigens, per preces solemnes institutionem Sacramenti et ipsa Christi instituentis verba continentes, panem in manus acceptum frangens, vinumque in calicem effundens, utrumque symbolum benedicit, atque in Sacramentum Corporis et Sanguinis Christi consecrat[2]."

In *Particulars to be considered* (no 57) Cosin suggests that a rubric be inserted, so as to give "better warrant" for the practice.

"No direction is given to the Priest (as in King Edward's Service-Book there was, and as in most places it is still in use)

[1] Cosin, *Works*, v p. 340.   [2] *Ib* iv. p. 359.

to 'take the bread and cup into his hands,' nor to 'break the bread before the people,' which is a needful circumstance belonging to the Sacrament, and therefore for his better warrant therein such a direction ought here to be set in the margin of the book[1]."

Again, in L'Estrange's *Alliance of Divine Offices* (A.D. 1659):

"By the marginal ascription of the 1 B. of Edw. VI. we may observe *from whence the custom is derived* for the minister to take the elements into his hands upon his pronouncing the words of institution[2]."

Both parties were prepared to welcome some clearer directions as to the amount and character of the ceremonial which should mark the solemn recital of the Institution. The Presbyterian ministers at the Savoy Conference urged this appeal:

"We conceive that the manner of consecrating of the elements is not here explicite and distinct enough, and the minister's breaking of the bread is not so much as mentioned."

Further, this remarkable rubric occurs in Baxter's proposed Liturgy, recognising both the lack of ceremonial fraction, and the fitness of some use of the words "Behold the Lamb of God" at the communion:

"Then let the minister take the bread and break it in the sight of the people, saying, 'The body of Christ was broken for

[1] *Ib.* v. p. 516. "Break the bread before the people" is the phrase adopted in our rubric. The Scottish Prayer Book of 1637 partly ordered our present manual acts, *but did not include the fraction.*

[2] *Alliance of Div. Off.* p. 317.

us, and offered once for all to sanctify us: Behold the sacrificed Lamb of God, that taketh away the sins of the world.'"

The restoration of the manual acts in A.D. 1662 was therefore a response to a widely felt need, and recognised that even the Prayer Book of A.D. 1549 was deficient in this respect. Several of the rubrically unauthorised ceremonies which had been practised by the Caroline divines were incorporated in the new rubrics, while others (e.g. the *Lavabo*) received no recognition in them. Elevation at the words "took bread," or after the consecration, does not seem to have been one of the Caroline revivals (although Laud was charged by his opponents with practising "elevation"), and the new rubrics of A.D. 1662, while carefully specifying the manual acts of the clergyman, do not direct any elevation at all.

The changes made in A.D. 1662 recognise and represent three characteristics in the service of Holy Communion which have constantly appeared in the course of this enquiry:

(1) The Eucharistic presentation of our gifts to God.

(2) The recital of the words of Institution with ceremonial acts which it is believed were those of our Lord Himself.

(3) The exhibition of the elements to the people at consecration.

(1) The first oblation, which in A.D. 1549 had consisted in "setting both the bread and wine upon the altar," but which had been omitted in A.D. 1552, was now restored *so as to embrace all the offerings of the people*. For the first time in the reformed service "the alms for the poor and other devotions of the people" were to be "reverently brought to the priest," who was directed to "humbly present and place (them) upon the holy Table." The order of A.D. 1549 was strictly followed in the case of the elements—"And when there is a communion, the priest shall then place upon the table so much bread and wine as he shall think sufficient." The prayer which follows, in which "our alms and oblations" are, together with our "great intercession," offered to the "Divine Majesty," seems intended to restore generally the primitive offering of all the gifts. The reception of those gifts, including what was to be used for communion, by the minister, and the placing of them upon the holy Table, seems to have been the earliest form of the Offertory-Oblation[1].

(2) The manual acts at the recital of the Institution were restored and enlarged. Our Lord's own action in "taking" the Bread and Cup was again recognised, as in A.D. 1549. Fraction, which had long

[1] The words "humbly present" have led to a lifting up of the "alms ..and other devotions of the people" before placing them upon the Table.

IV] BOOK OF COMMON PRAYER 179

died out at this point of the service, but which had been adopted by men like Cosin, and suggested by Baxter, was now enjoined as another of the acts which we know was practised by our Lord. Moreover the "blessing" named by Cosin (p. 175) found visible expression in the Priest's laying his hand upon the Bread and Cup at the words, "This is My Body," "This is My Blood[1]." The act of "taking" the elements in itself involves a slight lifting up of the paten and cup from the Holy Table, but no further elevation is enjoined It is unlikely that a ceremonial act so liable to be confused with the Roman elevation would have been contemplated by the Revisers of 1662.

(3) The manual acts are directed to be visible to the people. The note of publicity is struck in the new rubric prefixed to the "Prayer of consecration," in which the Priest is bidden "standing before the table" so to order the Bread and Wine "that he may with the more readiness and decency break the Bread before the people and take the Cup into his hands." The consecration with its significant ceremonial was to be visible to the congregation as a representation and memorial of the great central act which we commemorate[2], and the object which, with widely different

[1] Our Lord Himself sometimes accompanied His blessing with this outward action, which however is not named in the recital.

[2] Archbishop Benson strongly presses this "openness" in the Lincoln Judgment (1894) : He says :

"The Rubric does provide 'that the priest may with readiness

shades of intention, both the Eastern elevation, and the Western elevations both after consecration and at the close of the Canon, had in view, was thus attained. It is the Anglican expression of that "elevation or showing to the people," which was forbidden in A.D. 1549 on account of its close association in the minds of the people with the mediæval conception of Eucharistic worship. The "breaking the bread before the people" represents that purpose of which elevation, in some of its forms, had been the exponent.

Thus although elevation, through its association for several centuries before the Reformation with a doctrine and devotion distinctly repudiated by the Church of England, is nowhere mentioned in our rubrics, yet the main ideas which it was originally intended to express are recognised in them, and form part of the

and decency break the Bread, and take the Cup into his hands.' The word 'readiness' relates to his own convenience, the word 'decency' to the becomingness of the action in the eyes and view of the worshippers. Books of devotion frequently desired communicants to fasten their eyes upon these actions of the priest. To hide them would be as if the signing of the child with the Cross were hidden in Baptism. The significance of those acts being open lies in what was the principle from the beginning, however overlaid at times. The Consecration consists in the rehearsal and repetition of what the Lord did and said If any ceremonial is to be visible to the People, that Action of Christ unquestionably ought to be so by the rule both of the Gospel and of our Prayer Book." *Reid v. Bp of Lincoln* (Macmillan), p. 51. See also p. 52. The parallel case in Baptism would rather be the actual Baptism with water in the name of the Holy Trinity. The quotation from the rubric is not exact, the words "before the people" being omitted.

devotional thought of our service. For we find in these restorations of A.D. 1662 the acceptance of the two principles which this ceremony has been generally taken to signify—(1) that of presenting our gifts to God as representing our *Eucharistia* for His acceptance and blessing, (2) that of presenting the consecrated Bread and Wine to the people as the witness and memorial of the " precious death and bloodshedding " of the Redeemer.

Viewed in this light the last revision of the Book of Common Prayer restored to our Church a complete representation of what our Lord is recorded to have said and done " in the same night that He was betrayed." We " take the Bread " and " take the Cup " as He Himself did, we say the words of Institution which we believe that He said, we break the Bread and bless the Cup as He did, and we perform these significant actions openly in the sight of the people and thus " proclaim the Lord's death till He come."

INDEX.

Addis and Arnold, 69
Adoration to *follow* not *precede* consecration, 79, 145 f.
Agnus Dei, 62
Alcuin, 87
Alexander of Hales, 114
Alphabetum Sacerdotum, 68, 80, 93, 110
Amalarius, 13, 16, 65 f., 87 f., 101, 151
Ambrose, St, 57
Anastasius Sinaita, 48
Ancyra, Council of, 11
Andrewes, Bp, 171
Apostolic Constitutions, 10, 18, 22, 22 f., 36, 50, 135 f.
Aquinas, Thos., 114
Augustine, St, 57, 85
ἁγιάσας, 19 f.
ἅγιοι ἔσεσθε κ.τ λ., 41
ἀναδεικνύναι, ἀνάδειξις, 21—26, 45
ἀναδείξας σοὶ τῷ θεῷ, 19, 22
ἀποφαίνειν, 23

Bangor, Use of See *Missals*
Basil, St, 17, 23—25
Basnage, S., 46
Baxter, R., 62, 176 f.
Becon, Th., 95

Bellarmine, Card., 24, 57
Bell-ringing, 104, 125 f.
Bema, The, 52 f.
Benediction, Service of, 128
Benson, Abp, 62, 179 f.
Berengarius, 102, 127
Bingham, J, 25, 50, 57
Bishop, Mr E, 126
Blunt, Rev. J. H., *Dict. of Theol.*, 161
Bona, Card., 6, 30, 46, 57, 86 f
Bonaventura, St, 53, 152 f., 157, 163 f
Brandenburg-Nuremberg Service, 137
Brightman, Rev. F. E, 10, 11, 12, 15, 19, 21 f, 25, 35, 43 f., 46 f., 48, 51, 72
British Museum, Coins at, 154 f.
Burckard's *Ordo Missæ*, 69, 81, 93, 111, 119, 123

Canons, Extracts from English, 131 f.
Carthusian Statutes, 80, 103, 118
Ceremonial, development of, 124 —130
Ceremonies and Rites, 1 f.

INDEX

Chalice, lesser elevation of, 113—124

Chambers, Mr, 154 f.

Chasuble lifted, 111

Chrysostom, St, 16, 33, 40, 54, 57, 85, 87

Cistercian Chapter, 104 f.

Clement, St (Alex.), 13

Clement, St (Rome), 10

Coins, Chalice and Host on, 86, 154 f.

Colet, Dean, 161

Commixtio, 37, 61 f.

Common Prayer, Book of, A.D. 1549, 32, 61 f., 82, 112 f., 137, 167—170, 174; A.D. 1552, 167 f., 171; A.D. 1662, 21, 71, 82, 171—174, 177 f.

Communion, Order of, 166

Confession of Dositheus, 56

Confessio Orthodoxa, 56

Consecration, where placed, 13; Apostles and Prophets supplied "Word of God" in, 20; within *Bema*, 53 f.; distinction between "offering" before and after, 172

Consistentes, The, 36

Creed, Nicene, in Mozarabic Use, 36, 97 f. ; genuflexion in, 129

Consuetudinary, *Sarum*, 117

Corpus Christi, 127

Cranmer, Abp, 61, 137

Crossings, The, 84 f., 88, 90 f., 94, 99, 153

Cup, caution in elevating the, 75, 113 f.

Cyril, St (Alexandria), 22, 34

Cyril, St (Jerusalem), 11, 18, 31, 33, 40

Cyril of Scythopolis, 34, 46

de Cantelupe, Walter, 107

de Moleon See *Le Brun des Marrettes*

de Vert, 92

Dict. Chr. Ant., 44, 47, 50, 52

Didache, The, 14, 20, 32, 35

Didascalia (Arabic), 53

Dionysius Areopagita, 25, 45

Dionysius Bar Salibi, 49

Directorium of Ciconiolanus, 53, 68, 130

Dowden, Bp, 71, 173

Duchesne, Mgr, 54, 65, 72, 85, 88, 96

Durand, Ursin, 92

Durandus, W., 79, 112, 122, 159

Durantus, J. S , 51, 57, 129

Ecce Agnus Dei, used at Communion of people, 59 f., 165

Elements, joint elevation of, 67 f., 99

Elevation, different forms of, 5, 30, 63. *Rationale* of, 6 f , 139 f., 149 f. ; forbidden in 1549, 161;
Bonaventura on, 152 f., 162 f.
"ut sit Deo acceptum," 76
at Offertory, 9 f., 64, 141 f. ;
at "Qui pridie," 12 f., 73 f., 142 f.;
after consecration, 100 f., 158 f.;
at "Omnis honor et gloria," 75, 84, 138, 151. Absence from English Uses, 85 f., 132, 153 f.;
at τὰ ἅγια τοῖς ἁγίοις, 30 f.;
at communion of people, 59, 62, 124, 165 ;

INDEX

Elevation, of Host, 103—111, of Chalice, 111—124;
standing at, 128 f.;
slight, 78, 80, 103, 108, 113;
not reckoned as "elevation," 115 f.
Elévation, la petite (*elevatio minor*), 87
Embolismus, 93
Entrance, The Great, 11, 12, 64, 141
Epiclesis, The, 13, 15, 23 f., 28
Eucharistia, chief thought in consecration, 13, 142; early use of, 14
Eutychius, St, 22
Exeter, Synod of, 125, 130; Roman Ceremonial at, 129

Filioque, 98
Fitzwilliam Museum, 94
Fraction,
primitive use of, 21, 82, 148;
absent in 1549, 174;
restored in 1662, 21, 82, 175 f., 179 f.
Freeman, Archdeacon, 38, 42, 44, 150, 156
Frere, Rev. W. H., 129, 156 f.
Frisingen, Council of, 79

Gallican Church, 101 f.
Genuflexion, 93, 128
Gerbert, 16, 17, 19, 87, 88
Germanus, Bp (Constant.), 49, 149
Germanus, St (Paris), 65
Gifts of people, offering of, restored in 1662, 171 f.
Goar, 46, 49, 52, 57

Gregory, St (Magn.), 13 f.
Gregory, St (Nyss.), 20
Guido, Card., 104, 106 f.

Hæc quotiescunque feceritis, etc., 102, 112 f., 134 f., 167
Hammond, Canon C. E., 21
Hereford, Use of, see *Missals*
Hermann's *Consultatio*, 14
Hildebert, Bp of Tours, 76 f., 144
Honorius III., Pope, 105
Honorius, Bp of Autun, 76, 144
Hooker, R., on Ceremonies, 4
Hooper, Bp, 166
Hugo de S. Victore, 91, 151
Humbert, Cardinal, 10, 43

Ignatius, St, 14
Indutus Planeta, 53, 68, 80, 110, 119
Institution, Words of, 13, 16;
ipsissima verba of, 16 f., additions to, 17 f., 82
Ivo, Bp of Chartres, 90, 105 f., 151

James of Edessa, 27, 34, 48
John, Bp of Avranches, 90, 151
John of Damascus, St, 48, 149 f.
Justin Martyr, St, 13 f., 20, 127

Khosroes, 44
Κλάσις and μελισμός, 21

Laud, Abp, 172
Lay Folks' Mass Book, 107 f., 126, 129
Le Brun des Marrettes, 88, 92
Legg, Dr Wickham, 157 f.
L'Estrange, 176

INDEX

Lightfoot, Bp, 10
Lincoln, Bp of (King), 62, 179
Liturgy of Abyssinian Jacobites, 36, 50, 136; Armenians, 44, 135; Coptic Jacobites, 21, 27, 36, 50, 136; Ethiopic, 15, 17, 21, 36, 43; Nestorians, 14 f., 17, 43, 50, 72, 136; Pontic Exarchate, 11; Syrian Jacobites, 19, 27, 36, 43; St Basil, 11, 19, 23, 25, 27, 36, 41, 50, 135; St Chrys., 10, 12, 19, 36, 41, 50, 136; St James, 18 f., 25, 27, 32, 36, 39, 41, 51, 72, 135 f.; St Mark, 11, 36, 39, 41, 50, 135
   See also *Apostolic Constitutions*, and *Missals*
Lombard, Peter, 114
Lord, Example of our, 76 f., 81 f.
Lord's Prayer, Consecration by, 13 f.; Elevation at, 84, 88, 92 f., 97

Mabillon, 101
Manual Acts, 82, 175 f.
Manual, Sarum, 80
Martene, 16, 92
Mary, Queen, adoration of Host in reign of, 129
Matilda, Queen, 105
Micrologus, The, 66, 74 f., 87, 89, 91, 101, 143
Missals,
  Ambrosian, 120, 136
  Bangor, 67, 80, 109, 117
  Carmelite, 53, 110, 120
  Charterhouse, 70, 80, 110, 115, 124
  Cistercian, 16

Missals,
  Cordova, 94
  Coutances, 68, 81, 93, 94, 110, 119
  Dominican, 70, 80, 109, 118, 128
  Roman (in Fitzwilliam Museum), 94 See *Burckhard*
  Hereford, 67, 80, 86, 109, 118, 129
  Lyons, 92, 94
  Nevers, 94
  of Pius V., 59, 72, 81, 94, 111, 119
  Premonstratensian, 94
  Rouen, 88, 92
  Sarum, 67, 80, 85, 109, 117, 161
  Sarum, 13th cent., 67, 80, 85, 109, 116
  Sarum, 14th cent., 67, 80, 85, 109, 112, 117
  Sens, 94
  Stowe, 61
  Ursinensian, 16, 78, 101
  York, 80, 101, 108 f, 117
Mozarabic use, 17, 36, 66, 69, 72, 96 f., 112 f., 133—138, 150

National Churches, rights of, 1
Neale, Rev. J. M, 43
Newman, Card., 83
Nicene Creed, Mozarabic use of, 36, 97 f.; genuflexion in, 129

Oblation, Words of, unaccompanied by elevation, 30
"Oblations," 6, 71, 173
Odo, Bp of Paris, 78, 103, 105, 107
Offertorium, 64, 66 f., 72, 88, 169 f.

Omnis honor et gloria, retained in Communion office, 168 f. See *Elevation*
Orationes super oblata, 66
"Order of Communion," 32, 166 f.
Ordines Romani, 65, 74, 85, 87 f., 101
Origen, 20
Otto IV., 104
Oxford, Bp of (Paget), 4

Patshull, Bp, 128
Peace Offering, 6
People, Offerings of, 10, 71
Pius V., Breviary of, 68 See *Missals*
Poore, Bp, 107
Præsanctified, Liturgy of the, 22, 42, 42 f., 51
Preface to Bk of Com. Prayer, 2 f
Presence of Christ in Eucharist, 83 f., 145 f.
Primitive Church, appeal to, 1
Prothesis, The, 10 f., 64, 141
προκεῖσθαι, 11
προτιθέναι, 11

Rabanus Maurus, 89, 151
Rationale (Durandus), 79, 112, 122, 159
Rationale (Cranmer), 70, 123 f., 160
Renaudot, 30, 49, 52, 57
Report of Royal Commission, 61, 131 f.
Reservation of Sacrament, 126 f.
"*Resurrection of the Mass*," 96
Ridley, Bp, 166

Ritus Celebrandi Missam, 59, 69, 94, 111, 165
Rubricæ Generales, 130

Sacrificium, The, 66
Sacring, Second, 95
Sala, 30, 46, 87, 104, 114
Sancta Sanctis in Mozarabic Rite, 36 f, 98
Sanctification of Communicants, Prayers for, 32, 35, 43
Sarum, Use of, see *Missals*; *Manual*, 80, *Consuetudinary*, 117
Savoy Conference, 62, 176 f.
Scripture, appeal to, 1
Scudamore, Rev. W. E., 46 f., 53, 56, 103
Secretæ, The, 66
Serapion, Bp, 15
Shewbread, The presentation of, 11
Simmons, Canon, 126
Soto, D., 114 f.
Symeon of Thessalonica, 49

Theodoret, 11
Thiers, 87
Toledo, Council of, 97, 127
Transubstantiation, rise of doctrine of, 102, formal definition of, 7 f., late acceptance of in East, 56; effect of on elevation, 73, 83, 104—108, 124 f., 158 f.
Two Studies, 13 f.
τὰ ἅγια τοῖς ἁγίοις, meaning of, 31 f.; response to, 36; translations of, 43 f.; Freeman's view of, 38 f.

τὰ προηγιασμένα, 42

ὑποδεικνύναι, 21, 45 f.

Valens, 11
Veil of Bema, 52 f.
Venables, Canon, 44, 47, 50

Walfridus Strabo, 87

Warren, Rev. F. E., 61
Waterland, Archdn, 145
William, Bp of Paris, 104, 106
Wordsworth, Bp J., 25, 146
Wren, Bp, 171
Wurzburg, Council of, 78, 116

York, Use of, see *Missals*

www.ingramcontent.com/pod-product-compliance
Lightning Source LLC
Chambersburg PA
CBHW072128160426
43197CB00012B/2032